Antérieurement, Maintenant, et Plus Tard ~ Then, Now, and Later: A Collection of Verse

William Howard Kazarian

authorHOUSE®

AuthorHouse™
1663 Liberty Drive
Bloomington, IN 47403
www.authorhouse.com
Phone: 1-800-839-8640

First published by AuthorHouse 10/14/2011

ISBN: 978-1-4670-2425-9 (sc)
ISBN: 978-1-4670-2424-2 (e)

Library of Congress Control Number: 2011916458
Printed in the United States of America

This book is printed on acid-free paper.

The views expressed in this work are solely those of the author and do not necessarily reflect the views of the publisher, and the publisher hereby disclaims any responsibility for them.

This collection of poetry is an original work of fiction. All characters, incidences, and events are either products of the author's imagination or are used herein fictitiously. Any resemblance to persons living or dead, or events, or locales is entirely coincidental.

The Cover Art: "Birds, Peony, and Bamboo" (38" x 20" Chinese Silk Gongbi Painting) by artist He Min. From the Oriental Collection of Dr. William Howard Kazarian, 2011.

Contents

"Writing a book of poetry is like dropping a rose petal down the Grand Canyon and waiting for the echo." Don Marquis

Life

Humor

Remembrance

Strife

Dreams

Youth

Religion

Places

Love

People

Open Cage – Empty Nest

Life

Optima quacque dies miseris mortalibus aevi
Prima fugit; subeunt morbid tristique senectus
Et labor, et durae rapit inclementia mortis.
All the best days of life slip away from us poor mortals
first; illnesses and dreary old age and pain sneak up,
And the fierceness of harsh death snatches away.
Georgics, iii.66, Virgil (70-90 B.C.E)

The Dove on the Lanai – Part One
The Dove on the Lanai – Part Two
The Dove on the Lanai – Part Three
How I Spent Sunday December 23, 1968
In Principio
La Propriété C'est le Vol!
Modern Times
My Reverie of Tongues

The Dove on the Lanai – Part One

All these many years I have heard and seen the doves in their peculiar dance of love
Their ritual of sexual consanguination and waltz but as they live, I am not an ornithologist
I have no idea what they were up to until they constructed their nest and laid their eggs
Tiny and delicate like pearls and as fragile as bubbles on the air living off a mother's warmth.

I am transfixed by the hen…if that is appropriate…who sits motionless hours on end;
And when she does move, stretches in an almost ritual way, her small body, her tail wings,
As if to signal some sea change…and her position in late afternoon faces east in knowledge,
Through natural recognition or maybe in some even more undiscovered scientific stagecraft.

Her eyes seem always open as if awake and alert; yet, her head rarely turns to acknowledge;
If by my accidental intrusion to water the plants…dying in this environment of giving birth…but
To her a mere annoyance or a higher awareness that her mission is greater than my simple duties.
Where she now in peace and genuine serenity holds absolute sway over this particular dominion.

Yet, here is the most interesting aspect to this entire brief and deceptively poignant cycle;
While it is I who furnishes the room, raises his own children in this so-called home…here one
Begins to realize that we now share a common relational set of order amongst ourselves
Like the gecko chirping unseen at evening, the spider hiding quietly, they who also live here.

Such are...at least for me...the very humbling designs of nature which in so many ways
Trick one into believing in a hierarchy...actually a man created system of order...and...
Manifested as a chart, say order of being, caste system, phylum, genera, and all other forms;
Biological terms and symbols we use to represent the others who so unlike us occupy this world.

But another strange thing, what experts might call an anomaly; this dove hen is quite beautiful,
Grey tinged with faint blue hues, neck speckled with pure white dots, eyes hazel and cobalt;
Though as tranquil as her heartbeat as if in solemn peace and pure and natural in her rest,
Her feathers immaculate as manicured vestments of queens and such whose beauty lies within.

In the morning she calls what sounds like rococo and in response, two doves fly to her with food.
I have seen miracles, the beauty of day, a child's smile, the birth of a foal, the joy of fatherhood,
All these rise to the unbound glories of life, I am now a part of this curious and protracted labor,
To me at least a seeming labor of love...displaying its own particularly unique journey of life.

I cannot help but be impressed by the ebb and flow of nature in its extremes of constant change,
Of the beautiful and horrible, of the birth and distinctiveness of its fury in love and chaos;
Or of its design or random careening across the aisles of time and space in a continual dance
Among the heavens and the firmament above the earth which is the genesis of this new life.

The Dove on the Lanai – Part Two

Often, and this is probably accurate, the main reason very few people become scientists,
I begin to understand; one egg, one very small bird known as the species *cŏlumba latinate*
Emerges from the lone egg as ridiculously obtuse and as abstract as a skinless walnut;
Deep furrows, brown stripes against a yellow form, nearly still, cowering in its weedy nest.

And what of me? As nervous as an expectant father hovering from just a little too far away...
I anguish over the survival of this far too small bird trying to survive bouts of cold Kona winds
While the mother scours the landscape for mutual sustenance; that word there for a recorded log
The clinical observer sits as still and waits like a surrogate parent to chart and graph and map.

A curious irony here, I begin to really understand the depths to which Burns viewed his *mousie*,
Its upturned *'wee housie too in ruin'* and both of us in winter again not known for its fecundity,
Or in any real context of regeneration recognized for creating and comforting any new life;
And blankets the bare nest with cold wind and spray of rain and nothing but the mother's wing.

So here I am a mere chronicler helpless in any way to assist nature, creation, nor solve and save;
It is a real pity to be and feel so helpless...as helpless as that little bird who shivers and waits.
Yet, if I should deign or dare to dig more deeply into the symbolism or at a minimum in allegory
What might be a metaphor of my own time, my own age, my own struggle for toward existence.

5

I will not write a final chapter or stanza to this unique saga…at least for me where nature is seen
In the wind, the sun, and the other forces that will write this poem better than any hand might do;
Nor moved by Erato, or by empathy…to be honest, written by the will of another who at the end
It is the mother who wraps her love over the tiny seed and prays like me to create another flower.

The Dove on the Lanai – Part Three

One of the greatest lines is that by Delmore Schwartz whose existence ended far too early;
But without the illuminating enigmatic questions of why, and how, and all the causal villains;
His writing announced a life which might have been rescued or redeemed or some way meant
Had he friends, family, and self-awareness to enrich, he would not have written about dreams.

The real irony which has marked itself on the episodes that occur rightly or wrongly in one's life
Is nefariously connected to religion and that is fine when that belief does not abnegate reality;
Or what is considered the temporal plane the here and now and we hope and pray we do not fail.
How can anyone define the world or nature sailing on the random winds of fate or fortune?

But when we are weak…as afraid, ignorant, threatened, and wanting a miracle, we pray to a god
As regimen, as transient as a migrant worker, a whore, a bum who desires and deserves better;
And when and if things do work out, we still cling to some strange and conflicted hope…a will;
A set of formal commandments that impel and compel us to behave in order within a conflict.

So, there it is…I touched the tiny newborn chick unmoving, mother gone, I feared it was dead;
I do not like death nor do I abide it wherever it is manifest as untimely and unwanted intrusion.
Now we may re-visit Delmore Schwartz or at least his words…in dreams begin responsibilities And therefore, because I fear…I shall never sleep. But still I touched her with a parent's caress.

In the sum of what we may be, I have no insight and I lack perspective since I choose to eschew;
It is by any means, someone's abstraction and other values that I will not invest time or thought;
The life of this dove I now might see as symbolic love and hope of life and manifest in spirit to
Cythereiades as sacred to Venus which by invocation joins the cosmic dance that has been played.

Always the nagging questions of what is true, what is real, what is truth itself in main?
So here is the conflict of knowledge and belief and science and what of hope and prayer
Our last and most important vestige of faith, faith that binds our beliefs on salvation, hope and
Prayer that might be the exact foundation of all our choices, decision, values, and failures.

As if in the fairy tale I saw this frozen newborn, feathers unformed, eyes like tiny slits, caged,
I touched it gently as a mother to give it life and hope and love to let it know the taste of freedom
That it could soar among the winds and over the vast landscape of sea and land and in its way
Visit all the pleasures that nature and destiny and man's divination into its symbolism invests.

How I Spent Sunday December 23, 1968

San Francisco – 8 am Sunday – Weather Report: *San Francisco Chronicle*: "Early morning fog followed by partly cloudy skies; a high of 53 and a low of 49, skies clearing in the afternoon with light breezes from the west, sunset at 6:20."

Things to do:
1. Buy paper, markers, and tape at Owl Drug Store on Market Street;
2. Borrow a staple gun from Brian the out of work carpenter;
3. Enlist the help of at least three friends;
4. Map out routes that cover the Panhandle, north to Cow Hollow, east to Jackson Square, and south to the Castro;
5. Make copies of the poster where Jerry works part-time so I can get them free;
6. Distribute the posters throughout the City on utility poles, fences, buildings, and windows;
7. Go to Saints Peter and Paul on Filbert Street and do confession;
8. Devote much of the day to penance reciting over and over the litany of prayers such as the *Our Father*, the *Apostles Creed*, the *Nicene Creed*, legions of *Hail Marys*, and hordes of *Confiteors*...mea culpa, mea culpa, mea maxima culpa!
9. Catch the 39 Muni for the ride home taking special care to rub my knees which have atrophied by now;
10. Return to the beginning and do it all over again – this time without the Catholic remorse.

How to phrase my loss...
How to describe my loss...
How to post a reward...

Should I include a picture or will respondents heed the call by metaphysics or by Freudian angst, or by faith which has by now been ransacked by Viet Nam, polluted government, a poisoned society, the vast wasteland that is media, and the impending death of our own planet – an argument which will last for the next fifty years as generations sit idly by and silently observe the erosion – ultimate and inevitable.

Lost: my virginity and last vestige of self-identity and personal ownership.
When: around midnight of December 23, 1968.
Where: the corner of Haight and Stanyan Streets, second floor apartment.

Anyone having information about this item and its whereabouts is asked to please return it to any United States Post Office or donate it to anyone who has lost their self-esteem, is suffering from postpartum depression, is a victim of the pandemic invasion of personal privacy by religion, society, and politics; or, turn it over to any poor soul in need of reassurance, sympathy, nurturing, or a sturdy moral compass.

A small reward will be provided as consideration.

In Principio

The greatest confusion is related directly to what the first question is or more aptly, what is the greatest concern?

So here is a list which of course will require some adjustment as it moves along…or more correctly as the mood might impel this very uninspired dialogue disguised as poetry which might be prose that would serve as well as merely a list which is precisely what the initial intent was to have been if truth be known.

The litany and sometimes chorus of sirens of indistinguishable emergency vehicles propelling casualties, heartbreaks, and the steady flow of injured weak and strong, minor or apocalyptic to some cradle of humanitarian succor which would never of itself guarantee restoration.

The seeming incessant bravado of self-announcement heralded not by the dignity of a Purcell processional or an introduction by Respighi but the insouciant hiss and boom, deafening and maddening, as it makes no sense of *basso profundo*, sub-woof taken to *extremis* as if this aspect of technology held the grail of human salvation.

Or it might be the orchestral solos of car alarms frightened into their peculiar sonatas by movements of air, sidelong glances, an occasional utterance either by bird or dog or human, the passing of gas, the stare, the comment which carries no specific gravity but just enough of a whiff of the shake of imbalance which is only the very slight difference between *French's Mustard* and *Grey Poupon*; yet, here is the good part since subtlety is never a part of this equation.

The real shame of this particular deluge lies in the complexities of the twin engines of commerce and greed, where once the natural attributes of land and sea are now relegated to the quickly metastasizing effluvia – the molten magma that was the glory of the genesis of these islands but now so rudely and swiftly replaced by the sick pox of the new leprosy which has populated the world in main.

As it goes, on and on, irrevocably, like a foul parade of a cyclic anomalies winding their way through every intersection of the valleys and the mountains and the shore and all the heretofore screed shoals defined by rents, lease-holds, and area names all vainly attempting to identify or dignify or somehow quantify some property not yet tainted or touched by the red tide of modernity that is crime – of greed, and arrogance, odd disrespect and contempt, of drugs and human failure, of the systemic collapse of the institutions, of failure of values and the collapse of all pandemic operations rendering in due time a sort of die off resembling a lunar landscape as vastly immense and void of art, music, and literature, the conditions which would otherwise make a humanity a gift from on high.

Perhaps at this point, a time for what none may call a final chapter… and here at least for me…I who pen these words and thoughts…I have to query "and where now go I"…and if this appears to any a weighty question or a most poignant decision and what I have heard called a pregnant thought or pause, it really is not given the constant aria of traffic and high speed elevated rail, the adulterous palaver of media trash, the truly noisesome zeitgeist of politicians so inept that they are relegated to such a low estate, and lastly, the blurring of values and constant hiss as an atomic pile unattended.

Here, as it must be, I will draw to an end my complaints, because that is precisely what they are and ought to be viewed as…a sad recollection of what this petty life was like for so many years and how that environment eroded not by orogentic shifts or movements of tectonic plates nor by any astrophysical changes, nor even the human uprisings that have often marked the great subdivisions of both human history and geologic time – but here I stand – chronicling what I pray might be the log of my journey across the seas away from this scoundrel island and to some new and yet unfathomed isle and unimpenetrated landscape that holds hope, energy, and the notion of yet a new personal discovery.

La Propriété C'est le Vol!

A very long, long time ago…what most would quantify as childhood but that designation would be both inarticulate and inaccurate for none of us – not a one – knows for any speck of certainty when we learned our ethical valences, nor how we learned them, nor if…and this may be the real consequence…from where the intricacies of morality and reality had their genesis…and as important…that chemistry or other physical or ephemeral venues made the connection.

For me, it began with the earliest of recollections of the sounds of the voices of the elders of those who had lived and nearly died the gamut of experiences from which many have lost all hope while some have risen toward an uncertain future built on hope, prayer, and toil… the elements of happiness which from a blurry, indistinct vision, or dream, or passion which fuels the joy of life that translates into family, fidelity, and the role of serving as mentor and model of those who survive and serve, and for the merit of giving respect nothing but the remembrance of their good name.

There is nothing remarkable in this allegory which is as old as myth, older still than the *Bible*, older still than tales and deeds shared around a primordial fire guided by ancient stones, charred bones, the remains of a tree no longer a part of the flora its distant past a part of ecological extinction…where the dynamics of the earliest lore began; so old those tales of everyday survival now became adventure and lessons to those younger generations who might follow the wake of the disordered cultural community slowly forming and deifying into a humanistic system…a totemic charter of a rudimentary guide toward the search for balance…and for meaning.

To me at least is the central question of how the selection of ethical choices…and I am talking about the primary life choices…how an individual arrives at these…or what impels one and such to make these decisions which of course ladder and bridge one another connecting inexorably to some finite position which is by its own design determined to be something material…whether as social position, physical gain, erotic pleasure, giddy wealth obtained in power, or in some other – unknown to me – sense of joy, pleasure, or reconcilable ranking. For reference, one need only examine the tawdry, empty exhibitionism of the notable greats of any empire now fallen and laid to waste in the so-called dustbin of history like so many clusters of dirt and lint hurried up in their frenzied march to Armageddon.

And what are my credentials? Meager, small, wisps of a child's garden of remembrances as told as lovingly as love from grandparents whose lives seemed to depend upon the telling...as they would underscore their own journey of survival to provide a bolder reality passed along to the next generation in the hope that this lore would serve to build and support the spiritual body...so much more significant than the physical...as if these would-be sages could possess a special knowledge about life; yet, the failure so prominent in some that lay in the simple desire of material gain...the physical entrapment of what is felt, seen, and weighted as the lore of the earth itself.

So, as I remember, with the tears of the great allegorical stories of the *Old Testament* anchored in an incredibly large and ornate book echoed every inexorable Sunday at St. Paul's Armenian Apostolic Church which was the fitting repository of the antiquity, of the ages, the aromas of long absent unctions, the music of language as embedded into primordialism as the petroglyphs of Lascaux, darkly arcane in raiment of the robes and mitre of ancient priests, white beards flowing like the ice-capped waters that feed Lake Van with their counterpart in a chorus of women whose life histories exceeded the expectations of biological fact and statistical probability uniformly dressed in their black crêpe and wailing anthems of unbearable misery.

Yet, if there is a salvation in all of this leaden drama for one and such as young as I for at that time, I was obedient, clean of heart, pure of soul as most certainly full of grace that time encompasses many experiences some of which are always – especially the precarious events – are always viewed in the parallel and vicarious stories of the *New Testament* which by most standards is a primer for those who are not old enough to have sinned too deep and darkly Dante-esque a proportion nor cursed God to the near measure as narrated by Milton or those whose lives have not ventured any farther than the limits of what formerly, church, and unseen yet compelling forces – each in equal competition with the other – the native ethnic cultural assets stamped on the memory like an indelible code and the impelling draw of an invisible and requisite need to assimilate – no less a cataclysmic surge of such a magnitude of the creation of land masses or say the origin of the flood.

There are – and I have learned this over many years – an infinite number of ways some of us learn and adapt and increase our own knowledge not so much based upon trusted lore but upon notions of instinct of survival – those same issues as reflected in the lore of the *Bible* as well as the reality of the narrative of old women – with their stories of pain and angst in perilous journey. This might be what could be considered the impetus for the gathering, the collecting, the wanton amassing of material relics in that they might in some way mark our historical events…as tragic, triumphant, and foolish as these might be but constructs of a sort of vestigial celebration…a creating of a storehouse of treasures sometimes nostalgic as reminders of our youth or as much those areas in our lives which were marked by a poverty not so much of physical wealth, but rather born of a more mysterious shadow of ignorance or doubt that might be called compensation for whatever elements were or one at times suspect our character and lived lives that may have been viewed as lacking whether real or imagined.

So that is the heart of this particular curse of human frailty which is most likely as paradoxical a set of traits as old, murky, and unfathomable as the deeps of the ocean or the volcanic arteries that vent and shift the equally puzzling mantle…yet unlike these geologic issues are the less explored areas of our own ghostly behaviors to which we relegate our ignorance under the label of conundrum – which may explain why the human need for validation seeks and hopes to find confirmation in the sheer gathering of the physical elements – the things which we hope will represent to us and others who we think we are, who we desire to be, and shamefully who we hope others will see us as is such a perspective, insight, and reality are true.

The ensuing phases could best be categorized as neatly if such were possible under the heading of definition, characterization, and legacy, this last being most forlornly telling regarding the issues of poverty and materialism – which is exactly what this essay to myself is all about – ownership, materialism, and the absolute reckoning of an inventory of flotsam as vile and useless as that amassed by the not-so-fictional *Citizen Kane*; although, the only statuary consisted of plaster bust of Mozart and Beethoven, on the obligatory spinet piano, paintings and prints worth maybe twenty or thirty dollars and other artifacts as useless and psychologically intriguing as the unknown citizen found smothered amidst a pile of *New York Times* bundled neatly as Greco-Roman columns dating back to the 1920's in a corridor of his family's brownstone on the upper west side lying uniquely helpless and as anonymous as any dead end slattern sprawled lazily and as destitute on a Red Hook pier.

In the summing up – an ironic title which I will visit in a couple of lines – it could be the notion of possessing things is a way in which we endow those items – whatever they might be – with our own selves like traditional iconic vestiges such as portraits, clan symbols, totems, even those meager and simple artifacts of status – licenses, credentials, crests, medals, trophies, the entirety of all those material representations that one hopes will serve as some kind of posterity – the name or reputation whether etched or inscripted in granite, reposing in a library or museum, a crypt or a mausoleum somewhere in both time and place to serve as some sort of bench-marker or epitaph or remembrance that now and then is taken down from the metaphorical shelf or altar to be examined and revered and yet, somehow and almost always, the materialistic engines of a primitive and little understood desire to leave a part of ourselves upon such a vast world and seeming endless span of time to be there – etched, sold, maintaining some mystical and sadly self-vaunting assertion of our desire for entitlement and lamentably, all of this, like dreams, hopes, desire, and eternal prayers for either redemption or remembrance or both for some miscalculated legacy or a wan belief of immortality...

So now is the point at which the summing up should take place – what some might envision as a premature and immature view of what one's life might really be about...the irony of confusion and ignorance – and the ultimately disgraceful act of overwhelming egocentricity – that would be the foul and corrupt seed of the magnitude and depth of sinfulness of pride, of lust, of envy, of covetousness – the very commonplace sins which are the plagues that lie at the core of our frailty, stupidity, selfishness, and the terrible innocence that masks any ability to discern right from wrong, good from evil, labor from sloth, honesty from duplicity, hope from despair, and charity from self – and so it ends and now and once and forever.

*Pierre-Joseph Proudhon: "Qu'est-ce que la Propriété? (1840); Property is theft.

Modern Times

I got me a good job at *Speedy Mart*; I used to work at the *Burger King* down at the end a' town,
But there was too much to remember; I couldn't keep up; I thought I could handle all the...
What did they call it? Oh yeah...multitasking.

I come from a family where we was all workin' at *Ford*, grandpa who knew stills, pa who could
Beat steel as well as he beat us young-uns' but that changed a while back when my line was...
How did they call it? Oh yeah...phased out.

I had me a wife and a coupla kids and we was all workin' real hard; me at the *Jiffy* fillin' station and the old lady...heck, she's just now bout' turn twenty, cleanin' tables at *Mae's Café* until...
What was it happen? Oh yeah...we hit an economic downturn.

I been nursin' a coupla *Lone Stars* an' lissenin' to the Oakridge Boys an' they's back least-wise
On my country station which I remember good cause I got rid of the knobs an' I been thinkin'...
What was they say that? Oh yeah...I oughta' diversify.

I 'spose tomorrow I'll put on my wife's pantyhose to cover my face and go strapped with my Raven 25 which I'm holdin' for my friend Rufus who's in county for theft an' arson so I can...
How was it explained? Oh yeah...seekin' new niches for self-enrichment.

My Reverie of Tongues

I have long thought how wonderful it would be to have what can be considered a special gift
The ability to speak whatever language when one wanted and that at will and without effort.

Most of us as children wish to fly...flit like the robin or soar like the seagull or wholly possess
The territorial expanse of land or an eagle or of the oceans like the sea-going albatross of lore.

And who as a child has not wished himself an owl...wise and rapacious, or a crow with a legacy
His special thievery, or a simple, noisy mynah strutting with no noble purpose or self-awareness.

We children lying on our backs on the fresh mown lawn gazing idly at the sky as we have done
Making pictures and images of clouds and wondering we might be mighty lions of the savannah.

Or the stilted Ibis wading patiently among reeds as ancient as antiquity...pecking at still waters.
Our youthful bliss unappreciated nor realized since none from without would dare disturb such.

We, who in our youth would dream the imagination unbridled in a universe we knew so little of
Unfettered by knowledge, education, and strife which now in age do a disservice to our dreams.

Newly Minted Orphans: Thoughts on Haiti

A half a dozen children all in a row
Sitting side by side in their little bungalow;
Playing and laughing and little do they know
That soon they will be orphans drowning in the flow.

Five little babies strewn about the street
Lying oh so helpless among the peoples' feet;
Crying there and aching and hoping for retreat
Dying even now as they have no food to eat.

Four tiny waifs huddled in the clay
Wondering and curious are they about their day;
Worried who might chance to come along and stay
And give them faith and charity and time enough to play.

Three small kiddies each cloaked in dirt
Pants so torn no shoes to wear and nary one a shirt;
Asking who will feed them while in such a terrible hurt
Searching for their mother who wore a dotted skirt.

Two small creatures crying in a pile
Watching strangers pass by their waste-filled little isle;
All alone and praying among the shattered tile
Hoping someone rescues them in a little while.

One last infant who's left to fare nowhere,
Barely understanding why no one's there to share;
Wondering how the world could be so angry and so bare
That life could be this short with little left to spare.

Newly minted orphans, all in a row
With empty hearts and empty lives here show;
The earth laid waste no longer offers them a glow
Their hopes of joy and love are now reduced to woe.

And if by chance could hear their prayer
Would voices rise and provide their share;
To make the cruel for once seem fair
And change the world and show we care.

Little orphans one and each
Goodness, kindness might we breach;
So that you grow as you should reach
The highest that nature's love might teach.

Ownership

When in the name of stately plump Buck Mulligan was that most abstract and idiotic word ever
Coined into unending discourse of invention that not even its creator pretended to understand
Even worse codified both into a social value as well as shaped, as if air could be so gathered
To form itself and become regulated into canon in the context of economy and human structure.

I suspect that most, if not all, the incongruencies that continue to plague the panoptic systems
Those that have grown over centuries has actually multiplied into a kind of delusional or maybe
At the same time a completely metastasized form of cancer that is slowly eating away at itself as truly as a historical celebratory parade down every main street of every pre-fabricated village.

Words, as well I know and understand, are abstract and change their intent when the context suits
Or as those who wield a certain power can direct their intent; there will be those who will believe And be swayed by the speech whether eloquent or inane and become so enamored and moved
Solely by blind hatred or by a fiery flow of vile rhetoric that damns the truth and praises the lie.

So perverted are the social constructs peopled by those who self aggrandize through power
And through money and influence all gathering toward an inevitability as manufactured legend
Or physically through the erection of edifices bearing a name and serving no more significance
Of purpose than a tombstone that has inscribed some actual honest reflection upon that soul.

Within a last analysis there really cannot be such a thing as ownership nor should there be

Given the failure to serve even a decent amount of effort toward reasonable stewardship
Not just of self but as much of that for others and failing at that responsibility of charity
No one deserves to own words and their meaning nor possess the might of their strength.

As the world was created by fire and chaos, the final epitaph will be read in cold emptiness
Where will be no recollection or recognition of those whose flat existence and selfish influence
Are static and meaningless, what dream could have been a legacy of greatness, of hope, of prayer
That had things been different, then the meek could have achieved ownership to inherit the earth.

Politics and the Nature of Evil and Salvation

The world has not changed all that much
In say ten or fifteen thousand years
Or at least as the historians claim to measure both human history and
The attendant historical events...and then we have interpretation.

In my beginning, I had no concept nor had I any
Need for discerning whether or not I could
Attain position, status, recognition, or power or even at youth acceptance and familial albeit
Conspiratorial friendship –and then there is degree.

One of the most curious and seemingly unexplored
Ambiguities of social structure and how it is
Aligned and allied and compelled by ego along with physical traits of manifest power
Allied with ego and selfishness – but of course there is perception.

Probably one of the greatest discoveries in anyone's life
Are the various challenges that rise up unexpectedly
And to include those events which are both expected and accepted as a natural portion
Or phase of the living gauntlet – and then there is attitude.

What is unique about these personal observations
Is that they become tempered and modify their own
Value by the passing of time or the tempering of age and the peculiar labyrinthine
Vagaries some fortunes take – which are subject to one's unique consideration.

I will admit that I have read many books and spent what could generally be agreed upon
Several years studying and worse yet, will admit in what one might consider free time
I have easily invested the might of my existence

Upon charity – or a reasonable contextualization of what that might
mean.

Now is the time to begin to examine the real
Personalities that inhabit political systems
And they are manifest and clear in their own perverse
Perception of the world – that this image is their own.

And in these systems exists perversions
Of power and greed and self-aggrandizement,
Always the same formula of sideshow freaks
Which is of course – the usual suspects who populate a world of
crime.

The world it would seem is made up of
A preponderance toward an environment bathed in logical fallacies;
Some might consider actual views of some a distorted and
Ignorant reality –but in the here and now must be seen for what it
is.

And now it emerges…the conundrum…
The eternal question of what is truth…which must beg the question
of
Whose truth is true…whose beliefs will you accept…
And what choices will any of us make?

We know from history that we live or die
By our decisions which have their distinct ethical valences in our
values and our beliefs
Where in that perfect world we might live in truth…a term so abstract
and diffuse that
It resembles more a fog or some other non-descript element.

There is a type of comfort of going back to one's earliest recollections
not just to mother
And father, of grandparent whose remembrances flow and ebb like
the tides of the Nile

Of priests whose orisons represent a special ark of their faith where the word as in the *Bible* or
The *Torah* or the *Koran* like other venues have brought to us the truth on high.

Whom do we follow, who shall lead, who knows the truth...is it divined by revelation...
By experience, through belief...under mystic spell brought forward by fire and incense, chanting
The words of old grey-bearded sages...or by edict of papacy or other militaristic
Rule...or by what the archeologists interpret as the word was writ in stone?

The reality is...or truth be known...that neither the ancients nor we who now occupy a landscape
Detailed and limned with scientific credulity of proofs and equations and evidence which eluded
Even the celebrated among philosophers armed with a reasonable
And repeated gesturing of a body of knowledge still languishes.

In a sense, we are not in an infantile stage in terms of scientific understanding and logical
Uniformity in mapping out what may be honestly considered who and what we are,
What we are about and the greater query
As to what we might be...if such be the case!

Here is the greatest difficulty of all...and not just of humankind but of the discrepancies
Between reality and the spiritual realm...that vague environment that usually occupies
The idle mind, the restless should and the inquisitive heart which ultimately presents the
Difficult choices that separate all of us from doubt and belief.

Then...beliefs, tenets, credos, religions, philosophies, and all the other stale proclivities
Of social machination that tend to drive individual or collective spirits are in reality
So much *olla putrida*...nothing but a gathering of elements that could never make in reality
An agreeable feast either for body or for soul.

Now is the point to utter the conversation of *consummatum est* which by some statistical
Calculations that we now call measurements or more clearly what today is termed metrics
Which is some type of ersatz evaluation of historical events or personal memories
Held as gently as a child nestles a small bird yet as rigidly as the soldier wields his spear.

The specific gravity of the topics and issues raised herein require and necessitate
A deep and thoughtful look into several themes which have presented themselves
Upon the terra incognita inhabited by man...those strands so pressing and violent in every sense
That their history must be examined and, it is hoped, resolved.

Those of you who know history will fully comprehend the undercurrent of truth...
Hidden so long that it has become one of the sacrosanct components essential to most of the
Dime novels, films noir, and curious fascinations that have become a part of an entirely
Interesting fabric in a new world that is plagued as never before by radicalism.

Why? Well...therein lies the real beauty of the story; so let us place it in the context of the year

1943 an interesting age and as curious a time of war, intrigue, and mistrust...
A time before my own that I find interesting because this is the elemental point at which I
Have developed my understanding not just of history past, but of history yet to be.

****

So there you have it, in 1943, I am conceived...and if my math skills and the limited knowledge I possess regarding birth issues and the nature of sexual intercourse and my vision of the solemn epic journey among the competing sperm seeking that egg, then by my calculations, the event is a heralding of the new year designated by the Chinese as the year of the monkey.

As chunks of time pass along, there are few events to mark my spoor save the atomic holocausts visited upon the Japanese homeland to end the war, I can only imagine was mainly designed to create a much needed recess for the world to mourn, re-tool the economies and politics, and begin to amass new weapons and issues for war in Korea and other arenas ripe for subjugation and conquest.

Time in its continuum sidles along relatively uneventful save the small victories in education, or in health, in freedom and equality – which will never be full achieved – and the many other human accomplishments somehow in their way minimized by the equally destructive failures and shortcomings of man's frailty.

We can look to 1967 and specifically on the very first day of that year – the Sabbath – that I can carve a notch along my lifeline as my introduction of fire as I stepped into the Megiddo that for many of our youth was Viet Nam with its arresting narrative that at once bears no resemblance to war but more to that of carnage.

Those few of us who survived defined as clinically and socially fit if not philosophically able returned to a world forever changed with no glorious welcome, nor a sea of patriotic banners, nor the loving embrace of strangers or families in one chorus uttering in plainsong *"dulce et decorum est pro patria mori"* – but being greeted instead with a sneering disdain and an unspoken pall of shame and degradation that would hang as a permanent aura of ignominy and subverted evil.

Ensuing years were, for the most part, time spent for us transitioning away from the profane and toward the sacred as we sought out ways to find legitimacy and once discovered, adapt it as new clothing while we burned the vestigial remains of the old and explaining our histories in showers of lies of having devoted past time to travel, or study, or meditation stealing the mantle as metaphor as our seeking wisdom in the desert of devoting the years of unspeakable confusion instead within the muted silence of a monastery.

Periods of our personal histories often intersected with and shared their hallmarks with other events like marriage, the birth of children, the solemnity of the passing of loved ones, and all of the seeming immutable happenings which are a part of the ebb and flow of existence and as one grows older, it is hoped that there is a certain effect of renewal in what may be considered important ways.

What are these reborn and newly surfaced elements, one may rightly query? They are physical, spiritual, and personal achievements that manifest themselves in many and intricate ways but for one and each of us brings a reasonable joy and satisfaction into our lives and they carry their own intrinsic goodness and beauty while each and in its own way erases lingering clouds of earlier shames of ignorance and youthful follies.

These are the times I personally delight in most because they are significant and more a part of the self as a sense of survival and a partnering will and the indulgence of sheer willfulness in a desire to grow, create, accomplish and make a life of significance and personal acceptance and the rewards about which Mallarmé bemoans the plight that has consumed him in his final years.

"La chair est triste, hélas! et j'ai lu tous les livres. Mais, ô mon cœur, entends le chant des matelots!" The sweet poignancy and bitter desolation of the heart he must have felt at his own failure to *not do* nor act in any way to ascend to hear the sailor's song, to gauge that unknown foam and feel the crack and whip of the spar and sheet taken up by foreign breezes and venture as did the ancients upon seas of danger, of adventure, of death, and eternal glory and joy at having at last lived that life that must be well-lived.

Your Red Wagon

Every kid had one literally, but we of course did not know the metaphorical attachments of red wagons and what needs they served for it did not matter – nor does it now.

Some were "store bought" while others were hammered out of sheet metal, hard wood, and just plain fortitude borne of love to fulfill a young son's dreams, wheels and this handcrafted though not at the artisan level but put together like dreams during turmoil and doubt and of hope constructed of all of a father's love from a flotsam of scrap metal.

Oh God do I miss that type of love and dedication that had put together the dreams of that child…who seems to so rely upon that little red wagon, so easily symbolic of that child's journey embarked so early on the road or river or sky of life, because youth does not necessarily discriminate between the physical wealth from the spiritual valences.

When I grew older, my wagon grew too, gathering the ambiguous values of what are considered valued or not, and how those particular artifacts might or might not survive at least my own lifetime – unimportant and insignificant – but a factor nonetheless, that would if they dared still be partnered in my soul and shaper of my wit.

And when I take inventory of my red wagon, I have realized that there are and have been those relics which have either by design or by need dropped as of lesser importance; yet, more significantly, those which have lasted as old trusted friends or brothers in both times of conflict and of serenity.

Sometimes it seems something as simple as a child's dream or just a little memory can grow into so much more meaning than was maybe originally intended and what the adults might call as carried away but that's okay because that is exactly the very nature of dreams and recollections.

Here is where, at an early age, comes the real confusion and the one personally held totally responsible for this entire confusion so may I cite William Carlos Williams whose child depends so much on a little red wheelbarrow and yes that poem has always bothered me struggling to make sense of those lines.

So many impenetrable poems, poems so dainty and frivolous "I heard a fly buzz" the pompous, self-indulgent gibberish chaining recklessly words into meaningless muddle "mudlucious" the painful, endlessly long convoluted re-telling of *Genesis*, rambling and dark as Satan's heart the blindness that consumed Milton physically and symbolically.

Tables and shelves groaning under the weight of volumes which decade upon decade replicate as a chorus of singers praising to on high hard-bound anthologies which have ossified changeless within literature and worse have themselves become the chant of *cave ab homini unius libri** insinuating themselves into the groves of academe.

Marching forward, mechanical, and as seemingly unending as legions of mechanical histories and narratives now blurred and without meaning scarring forever the youthful psyches, despoiling the innocence of the uninitiated, propelling them unwittingly into the fray of inexperience brought face to face and one on one against a harsh fabric of reality.

If one by pluck or even by idiot and random circumstance that an individual might rise like a primordial bubble of air so long trapped within an impenetrable and darkly deep tar pit and slowly as time measured in geologic expanse should begin to develop, to create, to survive, to have assets, to break the old mold of standard canon and be born anew.

And if by chance, and opportunity, and hope, and sheer will could there be a new voice with modern themes and relevant poetic celebrations and a fresh music that at once looks back over the past and peers in youthful passion and considered, thoughtful pursuit toward a glimpse of the future – that might fill our red wagon.

Beware of the man of one book.

The Apostolic Faith Church – Moanalua

Humor

*The most perfect humour and irony is generally
quite unconscious
Life and Habit, ch. 2, Samuel Butler (1835-1902)*

Collateral Issues
Cool Things Guys Do Well
How to Define Men
My Christmas Wish-List
Oh the Wondrous Ways in Which Women
Say No
Paean to the University Fraternity
Revising the Poetry Canon for the Twenty-
first Century
The Rime of the Ancient Passenger
*Une Petite Poesie á la style du J.
Peterman*

Collateral Issues

Optima quaeque dies miseris mortalibus aevi
Prima fugit; subeunt morbi tristique senectus
Et labor, et durae rapit inclementia mortis.

All the best days of life slip away from us poor mortals
First, illnesses and dreary old age and pain sneak up,
and the fierceness of harsh death snatches away.
Virgil: *Georgics* (c.36-35 BCE), Book 3, Lines 66-67.

So relax, and take your time, tell your doctor about your medical condition and all medications and ask if you're healthy enough for sexual activity; don't take if you take nitrates for chest pain as this may cause an unsafe drop in blood pressure; don't drink alcohol in excess; side effects may include headache, upset stomach, delayed backache or muscle ache; to avoid long-term injuries, seek immediate medical help for an erection lasting more than four hours; if you have any sudden decrease or loss in hearing or vision stop and call your doctor right away…today you have options so when the moment is right you can be ready to reverse nature for your hedonism.
We alter our world to suit our needs which stand always and ever, in this time, beyond the rest.

Women with liver disease, women who are nursing or are pregnant or who may become pregnant; simple blood tests will check for liver problems; you should tell your doctor about other medicines you are taking; or, if you have muscle pain or weakness, these could be a sign of serious side-effects; learn more about plaque buildup from *arterycuredotcom* and ask your doctor if it's time for this elixir; if you can't afford your medication, this may be able to help. Look for sudden symptoms, stop taking this and call your doctor if your breathing suddenly worsens, or if your throat or tongue swells, you get hives or have vision changes or eye pain.
We change the course of the world to fit our plans above all else and those of fate and fortune.

Tell your doctor if you have glaucoma, problems passing urine or an enlarged prostate as these may worsen with this; also, discuss the medicines you take, even eye drops; side effects may include dry-mouth, constipation, and trouble passing urine, better ask your doctor about any prescription medicine used to treat depression; this medicine is thought to work by affecting chemicals in the brain – serotonin and *norepinephrine* – tell your doctor right away if your depression worsens or if you have unusual changes in mood behavior, or thoughts of suicide.

We innovate the language with diprivan, dociton, bricanyl, faslodex, naropin, and logimax.

Antidepressants can increase thoughts of suicidal behavior in children, teens, and young adults; this is not approved for children under eighteen; do not take this with *MAOI's*; taking this with *anasept* pain relievers, aspirin, or blood thinners may increase bleeding risk; tell your doctor about all your medications including those for migraine to avoid a possibly life-threatening condition; this may cause a worsening in high blood pressure, high cholesterol, or glaucoma; tell your doctor if you have heart disease or before you start taking this; side effects may include nausea, dizziness, sweating and may cause severe bleeding, ulcers, facial swelling, and blisters.

We re-create the entire universe to suit our needs and compel existence forever and at any cost.

This can lower bad cholesterol along with diet; adding this can lower fatty *triglycerides* and raise good cholesterol to help improve all three cholesterol numbers; this has not been shown to help prevent heart attacks or strokes; this is not for everyone, including people with liver, gall bladder, or severe kidney disease, or nursing women; tell your doctor about all the medicines you take; if you are pregnant or may become pregnant, blood tests are needed before and during treatment to check for liver problems; contact your doctor if you develop unexplained lung pain or weakness, as these might be rare but serious side effects; threats may be increased through continued use.

We design and develop the self-fulfilling destiny of life everlasting, forever and forevermore.

This should not be taken more than twice a day, as it contains *femodoral*; *femodoral* may increase the chance of asthma-related death; this is not for people whose asthma is well-controlled by other medicines; this will not replace a rescue inhaler; side effects may include stomach upset, throat or sinus infection, inflammation associated with *rosacea*, side effects may include stomach upset, sore throat, infectious sinusitis; do not take if allergic to *tetracycline*; stay out of direct or artificial sunlight; talk to your doctor if you have gastro-intestinal problems, or you are taking blood thinners or oral contraceptives as these can lead to serious complications.

We are the center of the universe, the god of the cosmos, and the silver bullet for all conundra.

Per istam sanctam unctionem et suam piissimam misericordiam indulgeat tibi Dominus quidquid per gustum et locutionem deliquisti – Amen.

Through this holy unction and through His most tender mercy, the Lord pardon thee whatever sins thou hast committed with thy mouth – Amen.

Cool Things That Guys Do Well

Burp words,
Pee their name anywhere,
Having the ability to make farting sounds with their armpits and
hands,
Triumphantly and constantly enjoying life instead of obsessing over...
you name it.

Mentally undress women,
Laugh at everything humorous or otherwise,
Eat or drink anything at least once in your life,
Live without crying endlessly over...you name it.

Put together a full course meal,
Cook all the disparate ingredients together,
Pay little or no attention to preparation and presentation
And enjoy the results no matter the outcome or state of soberness.

Do anything on a dare,
At any place, any time, and in front of anyone,
Performing whatever feat with the greatest of aplomb and grace,
While the level of drug-induced, alcohol related impairment has little
to do with judgment.

Enjoy to the fullest almost any event
Whether it has redeeming qualities or not,
Especially if it includes skanky women, brawling, and lots of
explosions,
And it offers the ability to allude to key scenes as one would reference
an epic in literature.

When achieving material success
He can devote time and effort into replacing all the toys of his
childhood
To cherish them and the memories they evoke and re-create so
perfectly

And from time to time travel along that reminiscent path back to simpler days.

Find ways to engage growing old,
Relish a full head of hair or celebrate baldness while equating it with wisdom,
Growing any kind of beard as a benchmark of newly gained authority and elevated status,
Smiling with an unrevealed knowledge and personal satisfaction yet to be shared with others.

How to Define Men

First, make no mistake that the designator for boys can be the same as men and the opposite, no matter the age…that is a fact.

Second, it must be noted that the male gender is fascinated by all forms of display from the prurient to the criminal.

Third, let it be known that gentlemen of any stripe have in common the same litany of media programs both vapid and stupid.

Fourth, these include but are not limited to: *Lockup Raw*, *A Thousand Ways to Die*, *To Catch a Predator*, and *Most Extreme Elimination Challenge*.

Fifth, men will watch programs conducted in languages totally alien to their education and tastes like *Soka Ga*, *Kapuso Mo*, *Viet Nam Today*, and anything on Public Television.

Sixth, although it is a little known fact, the majority of males watch television shows on *Oxygen*, *Hallmark*, *Lifetime*, and the *Home Shopping Network*.

Seventh, men gravitate toward vegetables such as jicama, arugula, and endive although they possess little or no knowledge as to how these might be prepared.

Eighth, men can and do weep uncontrollably at missed free throws, fumbles in the *red zone*, or a bobbled catch on a sacrifice bunt.

Ninth, there can be no greater misery than a man suffering the company of women whose sole desire is to have a meaningful conversation.

Tenth, like nature to a vacuum, men abhor cell phones, texting, *facebook*, gossiping, *myspace*, passing notes, *twitter*, and everything *Hello Kitty*.

Eleventh, CNN and MSNBC found that 50% of men claimed to be Christian while 50% claimed to be Jewish. Another 50% claimed to be followers of *Sin Sin the Guinea Lad*.

Twelfth, a survey conducted by FOX found that those males queried were not affiliated with any religion but indicated a very strong preference for the *History Channel* and Nazi footage.

Thirteenth, in strict defiance of natural selection and social order, men who consider themselves heterosexual admitted they openly accept the values and choices of openly homosexual men.

Fourteenth, all men whether straight or gay freely admitted they held a special preference for women who found one another highly attractive and displayed their affections openly.

Fifteenth, and most intriguing, is the newly discovered revelation that Moses had been handed a third tablet which contained additional commandments to which he objected.

Sixteenth, pursuant to declaration fifteen, Moses abrogated the moral laws against heavy drinking, drug abuse, whoring, and partaking in generally concupiscent college activities.

Seventeenth, there is no greater glory in one's life than achieving knowledge of and the ability to freely access 16 year old Single Malt Scotch consumed neat in the proper glass.

Eighteenth, trout fishing, bass fishing, deep sea fishing, catching nothing at all – the ultimate sublime entertainment where men sit nearly endlessly in a definition of heaven.

Nineteenth, items on the "to do" list include buy a boat, build a cabin, travel the Greek Isles, take on wood carving, art, music, and writing – and search for the meaning of life.

Twentieth, do not suffer fools, embrace your friends, believe that God lives within you, have an abiding respect for nature, and keep an unwavering faith in all that you shall do.

My Christmas Wish-List

Dear Santa or Surviving Heirs,

I would like to receive the following gifts to help me through another year:

Gold Violin: "Spill-proof Urinal" ™ @ $59.95

Medline Deluxe Walker Ultralight Rollator™ @ $119.95

Rubbermaid® Carex Portable Tub Transfer Board™ @ $49.95

Philips HeartStart OnSite Defibrillator AED™ @ $1,499.95

Medical Alert Systems LifeStation® "Help, I've fallen and I can't get up!"
@ $26.95 Monthly

Pride Go Go Elite Traveller Plus HD 4 Wheel Scooter™ @ $1,995.00

Pride "Elegance LC-560W 3 Position Lift-Chair"™ @ $1,230.00

Telescopic Portable Reacher – "TeleStik"™ @ $59.95

If these items are unavailable or deemed too expensive, please give me one hardcover copy of
Prescription: Medicide; the Goodness of Planned Death @ $38.98 plus shipping.

Thank you!

Oh the Wondrous Ways in Which Women Say No

Oh the wondrous ways in which women say no
It's like how many words Alaskans call snow.
Aside from the head toss or flick of the wrist
There's always the phrase "not now…I'm pissed!"
Or "I'd love to you know, but I am such a fright,
I really must wash my hair tonight."
But I honestly think you are such a dear
Sadly though my monthly visitor's here.
I'm a proud member of the lesbian crew,
Honestly now, I thought everyone knew.
I'm waiting for a call on my cell phone soon
And spending time changing my ringtone tune.
I'm in serious training and cannot deviate
Please believe me, it's not you that I hate.
Cha no ma, choi oy…I no can speakee
Excuse me prease…ay na ko…tee hee!
And away with no glance over shoulder or brow
She will leave in a huff even sooner than now.
Oh the wondrous ways in which women say no
It's truly a miracle that mankind might grow.

Paean to the University Fraternity

(An Introduction to Poetry)

There once was guy name Dave, who kept an old whore in a cave, she was minus one...

No...no...not right.

There once was a man from Nantucket, whose...

No...no...not proper.

I knew a young lady from Zealand, who had a peculiar feeling, when she laid on her back...

No...no...too insensitive.

I met a young lad from Church Falls, who used a wheelbarrow for his...

No...no...quite *outré.*

There was a young girl from Cape Cod, who thought babies came only from God...

No...no...very irreverent.

A pansy who lived in Khartoum, took a lesbian up to his room...

No...no...politically incorrect.

> *There was a young woman named Bright*
> *Whose speed was much faster than light.*
> *She set out one day...In a relative way,*
> *And returned on the previous night.*

Clever I thought but my girlfriend tried to help me become more sensitive and show me how to celebrate love and life and laughter but she gave up saying I lacked emotion and imagination and she told me she needed space and that I should pursue other avenues of intellectual endeavor.

Well…I was devastated, alone in my solitude a prisoner of self-imposed exile brought about by my dearth of sincerity, my lack of passion, my flawed soul, my inability to articulate words into emotions, my squalid existence touching, tainting and pushing my abject failure to show feeling.

I think I now know what it is I have to develop and what it takes to write great lyric poetry…it is the experience of anger, remorse, angst, self-pity, cholera, Beriberi, St. Vitus Dance, a visit from the monthly curse, plague, lymphogranuloma venereum, or the dreaded wrath of God on high.

Now I believe I have what it takes to write poetry that will stir the hearts and souls of humanity.

Revising the Poetry Canon for the Twenty-first Century

It is an established fact and a pretty firm opinion that poetry it in its most standardized format of dah dah de de dah de de dah must have a change if it is to continue to be a relevant part of the literary canon most notably established by dead white men and including a smattering of fairly notable women and an unlikely inclusion of people of color, culture, and conceptual differences.

Let us be clear in stating that certain poets and their works will not be touched by revisionist ideology; Japanese and Chinese artists will be left alone since they are inscrutable, the Russians too because no one understands them, and the indigenous people like Polynesians, Africans, and Native Americans whose oralistic traditions and cultural artifacts have long been appropriated.

One must never conscience changing neither phrase nor rhyme nor tilde nor umlaht of any edda, or saga, or plainchant, or adhan, or hosanna lest any infidel dare to defile what cannot possibly be understood without the aid of hard to find narcotics, impossibly difficult interpretation, and death-defying leaps of faith, or anything that has been in any way translated from its original.

Eschew such editorial violence too upon the Latinos and Hispanics whose work in all forms deals with suffering, pain, loss, and agonies worthy of the apocalypse and to whom ideological reparations have not been met; so too the Jews since they are God's chosen and therefore must be correct in both word and spirit, and lastly the fabulists since they must be considered liars.

It shall now be considered that the following poems, as part of the canon, will be henceforth and forever known under their new and relatively more hip and accurate titles:

Original	Revised
To His Coy Mistress (Marvell)	I Want to Get Into Your Pants
Ode On a Grecian Urn (Keats)	Graffiti on a Greek Urinal
Sinners In the Hands of an Angry God (Edwards)	Wall Street Grifters in the Big House
The Raven (Poe)	Two Pipes Good, Three Pipes Bad
Song of Myself (Whitman)	Hi There Little Boy!
I Heard a Fly Buzz (Dickinson)	I am a Dried Up Old Skank
In Just- (Cummings)	Who Cares?
The Road Not Taken (Frost)	I'm an Old Man and I'm Lost!
Metaphors (Plath)	Knocked-up and Nuts!
Meditation Seventeen (Donne)	My Seventeenth Acid Trip
Rime of the Ancient Mariner (Coleridge)	Stoned Again'
How Do I Love Thee? (Barrett-Browning)	How Much Money Yo Got Homes?
She Walks in Beauty (Lord Byron)	She is Chain-saw Ugly
O Western Wind (Anonymous)	Who Farted?
To a mouse… (Burns)	To my sixth Martini…
My mistress' eyes (Shakespeare)	My Boyfriend's Back!
My Papa's Waltz (Roethke)	Calling Child Protective Services
Aunt Sue's Stories (Hughes)	Growin' Old in South Central

The Rime of the Ancient Passenger

I am an ancient passenger and I stoppest one I see,
With weakened limb and bruiséd shin,
Now wherefore stoppest thou he?

I have a tale of *sturm und drang*,* of much ado and fuss;
You see sirrah, by my weary face,
I am forced to ride the TheBus.

The stranger now here taps his chest: "Now whyfore stoppest thou me?"
I will tell thee thus a tale of TheBus,
That one called number three!

Surely thou knowest the sign of three, the trinity and more,
Learneth ye well from this living hell
And avoid the blood and the gore.

With sixth-tenths of a buck and ill-fated luck, waited I so patiently,
Cloistered in concrete of shelter I stood,
For the land ark called number three.

In cool morning breeze and the whisper of leaves 'neath a cluster of night blooming cereus,
I searched and I paced and until at last faced,
With ennui I soon became furious.

But lo I see, oh can it be! the yellow behemoth I wait?
No, no, not yet, my foolish pet,
Mass transit is bound to be late.

The listening guest here taps his breast, "I must to elsewhere go!"
Stand ye fast, for it will not last,
Mine awful tale of woe.

*storm and stress

49

The sun didst rise above the crest, while out of the west came she,
That roaring, hulking, sulking beast,
TheBus that is known as three.

See now I board her gaping maw, go I into her womb;
So like Lascaux with petroglyph,
She's very like a tomb.

Signs and symbols are everywhere and everywhere I see,
Hand scrawled "wuz heah" and "I luv beer"
In TheBus yclept* number three.

Look ye how she rumbles now, down streets that bear no name,
With bump and grind and belching fume,
This she-craft hath no shame.

Beware ye churls who in her path do dare to cross and caper,
This churning, rumbling, wheezing husk
Will turn you into vapor!

The intersection looms so near, ablaze with lights so yellow;
Look out, look out – ah woe is me?
We've rolled across a fellow!

And on and on the devil's van in swath of senseless fury,
To some vague rounds with lurches and bounds,
Moves she on in frenzied hurry.

Remember ye of sardines and things, stowed tight like bright anchovy,
Chinese maids with brats in braids,
If there be a God, now save me!

Still more and more doth enter the bore, a dozen plus one-thousand.
Rage on you beast, we leaven like yeast,
Whilst I find a spot to land on.

*named

At last methinks I see my stop, eftsoons can it be true?!
Get out of the way you unwholesome fey,
I must, I beg, get through.

Ye dregs, ye dolts, decaying mass, aside and let me be!
To work today, I must away,
'Sic transit Gloria mundi'. *

Epilog

My tale is done, my song is sung, my plaint is full with sorrow;
I survived today, ah wail away!
But my fate lies with tomorrow.

For as sure as the sun doth set in the west, and the moon doth rise
from the sea,
I shall take up my place while pondering space,
To wait for TheBus known as three.

*so passes away the glory of the world

51

Une Petite Poesie á la style du J. Peterman

(L'année, 1942, le printemps)

As I glanced up from my *Pernod* and saw you emerge from *le Bois de Boulogne,*
The morning breeze seemed to carry you along as if to push against the winds,
Amid the tides, through the dark clouds and sullen skies that overtook one and all,
That lapped against our beloved Paris…

You were as purposeful as Sartre, as melancholy as Ronsard, as enlightened as Rousseau;
Yet, you bore the weight of years upon your soul…ignited with the passion of the saints,
As deliberate as the hand of Debussy, as hopelessly mournful as the life of Mallarmé,
That ebbed against the spirit of our beloved Paris…

And now the days of joy are but memories that gather dust in the twilight of our time,
Of times at *La Closerie des Lilas*, our moments at *La Coupole*, the fog of *La Rotonde,*
The pointless, meaningless *bredouiller** at *Les Deux Magots* with *les existentialistes*!
That swayed and flowed in the blood of our beloved Paris…

Your eyes now drenched with tears, your hopes now faded like childhood passions,
The dreams now consumed with terror as you wordlessly ask… "Is Paris burning?"
And if, in some day far or near, you might reprise that former glory of youth and hope,
To see the lights and hearts again of our beloved Paris…

You will walk *le Saint-Germaine-des-Prés*, dressed in our latest Maison Vionnet *Zazou* suit,
Made of 100% heavy imported Scottish wool, with striped cotton socks or meshed nylons;
Women's sizes: 2 through 18. Imported. Colors: persimmon, fuchsia, plum, indigo, and red;
Price: $199. Shoes, brolly, and handbag also available. *Trés chic, n'est-ce pas*; see you at *Le Pam Pam dans les Champs-Élysées et Boul'Mich - n'oubliez pas votre bicyclette...au revoir!*

bredouiller (n) = empty-headed, spluttering; jibberish.

Kawaihau Mānoa Cemetery – Mānoa

Remembrance

When to the sessions of sweet silent thought
I summon up remembrance of things past,
I sigh lack of many a thing I sought,
And with old woes new wail my dear times' waste.
Sonnets (30), William Shakespeare (1564-1616)

The First
Girls on Their Bicycles
Insouciance
Mechanical Engineering
New Year's Eve

The First

Her name was Marsha Kalisch…or something like that…her shiny curls.
It is difficult to remember back to the past and memories, but…there it is.

She was pretty in a way that most would not consider so at that young age.
But her beauty…and that was it…was as iconic as Annina in *Casablanca*…
The Romanian girl whose newly forged husband desperately tries… against hope,
To win the price of freedom by gambling at roulette…and losing at every turn.

Of course, fate rests in the fat and sausage-like fingers of Renault the ferret,
Farrari the jackal, and Ugarte recently dead…eh bien…c'est la guerre;
And the dreams dying…as the faded past blears like raindrops on a letter.
Marsha Kalisch was a pretty girl; sweet in heart and face and voice and eyes.

Still…over the years I have always wondered and…maybe even believed…
Though beyond belief …that she is there at the somewhere where we met.
Might that it be that …all at once she should appear …to make her walk or fly
Because she was that beautiful and deserving of that freedom as any soul.

Or she could find life and in my unyielding love consummated in pure joy;
That our hearts would obey one ideal so just as to live beyond the rest...
Or become as young love so undeserved be understood and so fashioned;
To unite or weave or just to dance we two for one more time as one again.

Girls on Their Bicycles

This is merely an observation for I am not an expert;
But as long as I can remember...which is a very long time...
Because I remember thinking the same thing when I was a kid;
This would place the time at say eight years old.

The first was a time of excited youth dashed by the sight of nuns...
Their billowing black habits flowing like a murder of crows;
While the next event was a schoolmate of mine along with her friend
Whom I supposed in the blur of their passing...but they were indeed girls.

Their lithe bodies rocked up and down in a synchronized unison of youth;
More like the pattern of birds whose wings dart and tilt to change their direction;
Not the movements of those mechanically practiced Olympic swimmers.
Ah...they were girls pedaling along as birds flying to an embedded destination.

And let me be very clear on this....that they were girls...who rode bicycles;
Their youthful bodies flowed in such motion which belied whatever their age;
Which looks to what really, if anything, does separate girls from women;
I believe it might be that quality of natural sweetness flowering in the breeze.

Insouciance

Nihil Obstat

An environment is a great deal like a hothouse or nursery, and it makes little difference whether or not the plant is exposed to light, or heat, or water, or much of anything for that matter since one can grow orchids without sun, mushrooms from dung, vegetables from water, and weeds without intent; and, it is well to note the wise who say: "the kingdom of heaven is like a grain of mustard" as so develops from the smallest seed and so does it fly as with the birds to places far and strange.

But I digress...my metaphor, at least for me, is very accurate since the garden in which I was raised was fertile in so many ways that I must narrow my own various experiences...and they are indeed various...to make any sense for you or me to make sense out of my own captured, sometimes genuine, oftentimes co-modified, at times held hostage, at any given moment surreptitiously held at bay by archetypes, molded from time to time, shaped by larger and looming social distractions, confined once in awhile by religion, prodded and ushered by socio-economic exigencies, and nurtured by squadrons of family most of whom have never pursued any unique artistic bent nor taken any chance greater than purchasing a Swanson's frozen t.v. dinner at the corner grocery on Judah and Twenty-Eighth Avenue.

There was nothing special in the formula or soil that served as the bedding grounds of my education, the seedlings on my intellectual curiosity, the vibrant and tingling emotional seismic waves of the yearning desire for education...not solely relegated to the ivied walls... but as much to a real thirst for everything that was ever driven into me to all that has been listed on the *index liborum prohibitorum* and all other banned writings where the back story and the original intent was considered field research under the guise of searching for and establishing what was known to be a real establishment favored by such luminaries as King David Kalakaua, Robert Louis Stevenson, and my particular quarry...William Somerset Maugham whose life I had made my personal hobby and of whom I had consumed with eager relish almost every work of literature from mediocre to excellent he had ever written.

My own personal journey was charted in a diverse and interesting manner and under the aegis of the Department of Defense which was my employer as I worked and traveled as a professor of English…a sort of wandering intellectual among the groves of academe and as Horace noted so brilliantly: *atque inter silvas academi quaerere verum.*

Therein lies the personal beauty of this segment of my life…a kind of government sponsored sojourning duty that consisted of an endless loop of travel throughout Southeast Asia, to the Middle East, to Africa, across the equator, to Australia and back to the Philippines, on to Japan, Korea, China, and all the classic haunts so famously storied in the deep and textured halls of literature of say Conrad, and Kipling, of my great friend and mentor Clifford Geertz, and the modeling of the pioneer Bronislaw Malinowski…although thinking about him makes me want to wash myself thoroughly… and the personal diarists, writers, poets, an oddly assorted lot of ex-patriots for whom exploration might better be defined as escape from their own definition of reality, known and despised, toward reality unknown, undefined, and wholly exploratory.

I count among these brave souls the likes of barbaric Henry Miller who found beauty in Maroussi, Nin who found whatever she looked upon, Durrell who to me never really seemed lost, Blair renamed Orwell who lived a kind of self-inflicted *Confiteor* dotted with an historical pathway marked intermittently with lucid reflections of his personal distaste for imperialism aligned with a strong sense of atonement for having been a somewhat willing participant within the eerie and mystical formulations of the world of the *raj.*

And then there was William Somerset Maugham, a feeble, effeminate stutterer sent to live with a vicar – his uncle – and his wife, the second, who was more a father to *Whitstable* than to any child, whose own personal history was fraught with all the possible terrors and flaws that might confront any hapless Dickensian waif orphaned too young, the hopeless child abandoned in the swirl of poverty described by Victor Hugo, or perhaps the oppressive starvation of soul and heart of the Chinese so poignantly chronicled by Pearl S. Buck…but again…I digress.

The object of my pursuit was vaguely based upon a clue I thought I noticed in one of Maugham's works called *The Trembling of a Leaf*, but then, even as now, I am not certain as to whether it was real or imagined as one of many interesting late night excursions into Chinatown…that incredibly seedy and greasy collection of brick and wood shithole buildings standing shoulder to shoulder where city blocks had twice before been ravaged by fires that only succeeded in temporarily ridding the area of rats…but like nagging wives and bad dreams always seemed to resurrect themselves and evolve into the same architecture of cultural, ethnic, and smoky disequilibrium that was always a permanent part of the between two worlds atmosphere of that particular septic relic of Honolulu or any other tired port city like her, as worn as a shabby whore whose life and memory are but vestigial remains of bloated sea stories stinking of cheap rum.

There was some trace of method to my madness although I did not see it as that so convinced was I…and still am…of the rightness of my actions which I honestly see as grounded in my own view of faith and my belief in the value of understanding – but here I am sadly misguided into my perception that intellectual inquiry is always good…like prayer or confession…or forgiveness where everyone – evil or good – can seek and receive redemption.

Yet, I was not on a mission from on high, nor was my intent to make any discovery that could benefit humankind or enrich the empty, thirsty souls of most of the world's populace which – it did not already understand – was living only as bacteria exist…on matter and free of any ideation or process of thought that might cause them to stir in any appreciable way…just participants in the shadows, dancing mutely in the background, owing nothing to the universe and leaving no mark nor meaning of whatever space or time they may have filled.

There was in my intellectual backpack an historical context, a seed of events strung together as loosely as a *plumeria lei*, but enough of that curious fragrance of interest and the unplumbed waters of a drinking gourd that reflects both the image of one's face and the face of the future – and that as might be written down – as fate but always the incessant nagging to discover the truth which really has no meaning so I suppose my quest lay more within the constructs designed by elders...those whose first foray into learning and insight were the oddest admixture of intellectual query and brash and edgy bravado.

In most cases of which I am generally aware, there is some sort of significant reward or gain at the end of the metaphorical rainbow such as notoriety...perhaps a book...the mantle of explorer extraordinaire...a prestigious degree conference...even some secret and personal satisfaction that spans the arc from the glow of accomplishment to such sublime inanities as the odd set piece, say an antique relic, a souvenir, even a meaningless shard as common in its day as a Korean bar hostess working on Keeaumoku Street plying her wares in much the same tawdry fashion that was *de rigueur* for the breezy, balmy afternoons in the Iwilei haunts marked by the subtropical neighborhoods of Nuuanu, River, and King Streets...the gaudy, gilded corridors of that particular Chinatown of 1917 which the random passenger ships plied their way from mainland cities to the swaying palms that beckoned strangers to that strange land known as Hawai'i.

There are many fascinating coincidences jarring together in this one hemisphere that writers like Maugham noted wryly and awkwardly... *where people put salt in their coffee*...that in itself not so unusual... where such visitors, more as uninitiated aliens experienced the clashing of images painted on posters and postcards and the reality of those real sights they actually confronted on purpose and to me, at least, there is little by way of surprise that these travelling diarists should inevitably find themselves fairly early in any day seeking the cool respite away from the heat and sun and into the dark and sheltered grotto of any one of the pubs, bars, inns, brothels, and makeshift lanais that lined the area near Pier 7, as if to serve as a symbiotic industry to satiate and fulfill the needs of a multitude.

I recently re-visited my original steps that I had taken so many years earlier as I strode out and into the heart of the city on a cool breezy morning where the usual crowds huddled around bus stops as if they were clusters of palms on a white sand beach where fetching young women were passing out tropical drinks – the kind with the color of fuchsia, topped with a glacier of ice, and covered by the *bona fides* of a tiny parasol – all this on Hotel Street which ironically boasts no hotels and in reality is little more than a thoroughfare lined with tiny shops selling everything from cheap souvenirs from China or Japan, and clothing – chiefly for women and young girls – most likely churned out in the pseudo palaces erected by and occupied solely of large extended Filipino labor families where the many fruits of labor are spun on daily, without the pesky nuisances of safety, quality, taxation, or licensing which, in this case, is the very ideal definition of a cottage industry.

Further along the way, I crossed Fort Street which is an example of a failed gentrification attempt toward diverse industry; but, instead could easily be mistaken as the *saimin* capital of the world…from each doorway a smell unique to the owner-chef and his signature cuisine which is a faulty and irregular composite of handed down recipes and the mixture of the herbs, spices, and vegetables available on that day…the pungent Thai, the fish blood smell of Filipino food, the constancy of fried Korean meat, vegetables, all and one viewed as the same…where one can see signs written in every language from Vietnamese to Sinhalese, where the disenfranchised wander aimlessly so much more lost and confused, unable to read anything no matter their personal level of literacy as they push their shopping cart in a non-stop dance in search of something to which they can relate.

As I pause for a moment near the "barber college" – I reflect upon the knowledge that this is a world in which no one really lives…they exist yet by a hairsbreadth…but this is not real in any sense more than a parking lot is open space or that an alley reeking of urine is a part of the great outdoors; yet, someone, somewhere, somehow, and for some reason has seen fit to intersperse the concrete, blacktop, bricks, and speed blocks with the green patch here and there, occasional trees breaking the chockablock landscape, statuary mostly consisting of gigantic lions, dragons etched like raised embossments on buildings, neat rows of antique lampposts as smart as a British Regiment of soldiers; yet, everywhere a toxic stench that remains a part of the compelling pall despite strong *Kona* winds, despite, attempts to mollify the area, despite the oh-so-human endeavor to mitigate the ugly circumstances.

Bethel Street is the essential gateway to this re-vitalized Chinatown where there is a magnificent structure that tries to replicate what may have been one architect's vision of the cultural artifacts of older Asian cities and villages, where the actual guts of Chinatown begin to echo the harsh and garish reality – even on this bright morning – the dull and pulsating glow of myriad small bars capable of catering to man's basest needs, those that go beyond the perceived pleasures of drunkenness…their peculiar names glowing as if written in some arcane code known only to the evening cognoscenti whose nightly pilgrimages are a natural part of this world…patently mysterious not by its mystifying and *illusionally* magical nature, but rather because it is only *illusional* and not at all real.

I forced myself away from the disturbing clot of failed ambitions, empty lives, unfulfilled dreams, the parade of wandering unfortunates…and after awhile, they began to blur away from sight and mind and they became unnamed, unknown, unseen, and slowly I began to envision an afternoon…say about three or so, perhaps a Friday as that day has been favored with its own local cachet declaring to no one in particular that this is idler's time, rest and respite from the weary, a declaration of freedom and independence from the ordinary task and toil of a mundane world…*pau hana*…oh glorious reconciliation between labor and rest!

For reasons unknown to me since I am neither a clinician nor a forensic scientist, nor do I possess any training formal or otherwise in the causal effects of human behavior, I have always been of the impression that there exists a very fine line between free will and fate; and, having that in mind, I deemed my own strange research more of a delight, a fantasy if you will, or at minimum an excursion into a non-spectacular hinterland more suited to rattling good story than substantive intellectual acquisitiveness and hoped-for earth shaking result that would guarantee for me a secure niche among the historical archives of anthropology or perhaps go down as one of the great textured deep probes one reads about in the famed ethnographies of say Evans-Pritchard or studies into ethnocentrism of Levi-Strauss... but such was hardly the case.

I was at the onset of my strange and somewhat confused pursuit still relatively young as college professors go and I was yet under a number of foolish spells...what I might justify as idealism or that I might rationalize as my period of assimilation a sort of bewildering odyssey not unlike that of Amis' "Lucky Jim" only with greater emphasis upon field study rather than the clumsy meanderings of socialization – and this foray posed no threat to my future in academia since it was more grounded in a Marx brothers setting than if by a more serious definition, *a localized, close-in vernacular field research* – just a lark when there was free time to piss away.

So it was during those times that I gathered about me...or more accurately, I was drawn into...a circle of colleagues with whom I shared like ideas, values, tastes, and weaknesses and these we would dutifully celebrate on Friday afternoons marinating our psyches in pitchers of imported beer that would inevitably lead toward consumption of cheap wine, reverie steeped in heated debate over pieces of literature or their authors or the personal voyages we made as graduate students in a sometimes loving...oftentimes, brutal pursuit of our studies trying our damndest to be pioneers, putting together our portfolios of dissertations, theses, publications, and ultimate reputations which relate almost in retrospect the same as pushing one's meager fortunes forward on the green velvet of the roulette table betting upon thirty-four red, my age and financial circumstances at that time.

It is written that you cannot choose your parents; yet, I have no regrets there…it is with question I move forward in asking how one chooses friends in which opportunity can lend itself as unwise a decision as turning to a life based on crime, or avariciousness, or worse, total abdication toward a life and philosophical tradition founded upon all of the worst, most violent and reprehensible behaviors that any man is surely capable of acting upon…and for my purpose, for any reason, and for any consequence; but, such vulgar indulgences are only used here for example, rather that imagining – let alone hoping or expecting – there should be at the completion of any research venture and partnership that bring together by mutual interest two explorers whose aim is loftier than sinfulness or worse…any arbitrary behavior that might draw such devilish conclusions; and here is the beauty of the seeming random pairing of friendships, associations, and those bent on dreams coincident.

It does not seem that anyone ever said life imitates art but Henry James who freely rephrased his own coined phrases from the *Bible* is known to have written…"it is art that makes life, makes interest, makes importance, for our consideration and application of these things"…although my personal favorite is that of Pope who famously wrote…"true ease in writing comes from art"…but the point to this has more to do with one of my colleagues in this venture to seek and find the actual bar of which Maugham wrote about in his obscure and poorly written story – more of a rambling set of observations – *Honolulu*; my friend in this journey, should truth be told, was an incredibly over-inflated, self-serving, ersatz colonialist who had somehow transformed himself either by will or by drug or by delusion whereby he constructed this persona…as he had related on many occasions…his immersion into the works of the cadre of literary sojourners of the nineteenth century; yet, not sated with only the writers, he freely admitted an addiction to Ronsard, Debussy, Verlaine, and all manner of musicians, writers, and artists who either in their work or through biography had injected him with their individual spells an overweening intoxication with places foreign, and it was at this particular bench marker that I discovered he had spent years of service in the Philippines where he drank deeply of both the atmosphere and the culture, in particular, the women whom he found jointly pliant and enticingly exotic – two elements which over the years had dulled his senses to such a degree that when he appeared in Honolulu, his wardrobe for the most part consisted of white espadrilles and white ducks, topped off with a large *Edwardian* era moustache and an impossible air of one to whom the entire world belonged – the only items missing were a monocle and a topee, and through it all, modernity and historical changes be damned!

For the record, not that any should be kept for that matter, my companion described himself as Austrian, descended from the Hohenzollern line whose most distinguished feature was the nose although most observers might note that for one, the nose had regressed into a glowing red bulb no doubt owing to the influence of drink and that otherwise one might instead point to more obvious traits such as fatuosity, a tumescent frame, a jittery gait, and a terrible sense of memory for his had failed him miserably on the first leg of our journey which was marred by a number of misadventures beginning with an onset of premature senility brought about by years of self-absorption and cheap alcohol – the latter entering dosages that increased in time and frequency paving a path toward a dark side of humanity that was probably and at one time early on, viewed as jaunty, humorous, quirky, and a necessary part of some entryway down a corridor to creativity; but, it now only served to add to a comic swagger and sway, an uncertain groping about for direction, and the inevitable loss of gravitas and ultimate failure of the uniqueness of charter – all faded into a kind of comical portrait that captured only the very worst aspects of someone in the last stage of decline…as one who has fallen out of favor with his admirers…had such and any ever existed.

The heretofore admirable quirks of personality – those traits that provide an air of character as noted as artistic, curious, intelligent, risk-taking, innovative, piercing, and, when viewed as in some way successful – *brilliance* – now began to fade like a dying light of an old and well worn candle or the lantern whose wick is so frayed it is incapable of holding fuel, or the pathetic and tragically sad loss of color and gleam in the eyes of one whose very existence is dependent upon both sight and vision, now by exercise of wanton disregard for one's condition of health in both self and soul has reached such a pitiable and dissolute end the wanderer who has lost himself so much in the world of himself that he has now become squandered within the world of the people around him; yet, still he is able to justify his lot as if it were nothing more than a precipitous transition toward some unknown greater glory.

It could be that there are so many elements that can have an effect on the human spirit and there are those places upon this earth where combinations of those ephemeral, chimerical, and cultural conditions can and often do converge as mystical settings...what in the Islands are sometimes referred to a *mana*...to which visitors and natives alike would show respect and honor lest ill fate should befall the non-believer...to which point one only need examine the wheezing occupants who inhabit tour buses, that visit the volcanoes, remove rocks as souvenirs, return home, and then experience the consequences of what their own mischief, imaginations, and unusual fate hold in store for them...so it was in this same serious vein that I was an observer *cum* researcher with the same kinds of cautionary provisions that have led bolder men astray and this was one of those missions about which I had little confidence unless it was either underwritten by the *National Geographic Society* – which it was not – or would prove to offer at minimum a good yarn, years of happy reflection, and a reasonable amount of laughter over good whiskey at managing to have survived yet another frivolous expedition in a seemingly never-ending youth squandered on a serious attempt to make sense of what I have long viewed as a world full of inequity and rife with absurdity.

My afternoon in Chinatown in search of Maugham's watering hole was not anything more daring than Stanley's so-called search for Livingstone who, according to himself and others who knew, was never lost; thus, I found myself walking at least three paces behind my friend as if I were a coolie wife or a Dayak nimbly crossing torrential rivers or scrambling across tree tops dodging and darting all the obfuscations of the realm of nature but here in this strange sea of alien figures and faces in the uniquely odd part of Honolulu flitting through streets, and throngs of people with their burdens of bizarre foods fresh from the vendors' stalls of moon-eyed fish, fish with teeth, fish that were flat, fish so bloated that they might explode... the assorted vegetables resembling more weeds and poisonous vines, strange languages with wild inflexions, clusters of very old women bent over grotesque, their crooked backs perhaps a symbol of their own antiquity, cackling and chattering in the oddest of mixtures of sing-song cacophony and repetitious choruses of *ayah, ayah* that filled the air already thick with incense and dust and a special darkness that confronted any white man who by accident or coincidence might find himself dismasted, and in the doldrums in the outré climes and intrigues of faraway lands.

And so it was I found myself walking *mauka* on Nuuanu Avenue as if I were on a *hadj* neither to Mecca nor Canterbury but to something I know not what; but still, there exists in the quest some trace of poisonous and tingling curiosity which will always, and no matter what, will forever yield an interesting consequence which one can read volumes of books that record the strange histories of man's chaotic movements in this unusual world and equally unusual times, and those which bore out the conundrum of our human frailty...the gateway was nothing less than one would expect of a saloon for this place deserved the title of swinging doors that had seen in its long history at least four generations of *Kama'ainas, Haoles, Pakes,* and *Kanakas* stroll in with the same shared notion of respite and swagger... to remove oneself to another place either geographically, but more significantly by proxy the favorite transportation being beer or rum or some form of gin, and that is part of the charm since very little in places like the Islands was ever uniform, licensed, approved, or produced as some kind of refined, codified, and universally accepted product...so I could see Filipinos drinking *Tuba,* the natives drunk on *Okolehau,* the *Haoles* stricken stiff with *Ginebra* all bought in a tiny stall at fifteen cents per bottle, all glorious in their drunken rapture as we entered into that very still and quiet environment where all were huddled sad and morose over their drinks, a Chinese lady wiping the greasy bar with a filthy rag, a hook where a hand once was, the patrons looking up to greet us to this their tiny refuge most of whom were missing teeth or eyes, whose collective personage combined to make a most unusual tableaux that could have been the set piece portrait of a band of thieves or gypsies or pirates, I suppose, as it was for the here and now of this place.

These to me are the things that make life so incredibly interesting especially when one such as I can enjoy a perspective as looking back on these odd occasions and having survived which ultimately is what counts because…as noted earlier…no one can claim the statement that life imitates art, so let me be the first and only one to declare with impunity, that art evolves from life as witnessed in this conversation that my colleague engaged with the bar maid…she of the hook… that he would deign to open this incredible meeting…a cultural clashing of tectonic plates with his awkward, base, and over-arching greeting of "my good woman" to which the bar lady responded as quickly and as naturally: *I'm not your good woman!* and in my mind I smiled at how clever of me to reply *I don't care what your past has been; to me, you'll always be my good woman!* But I did not.

Within the deep well of my personal knowledge there are circumstances which require a quick verdict; among these buds of wisdom were the *Proverbs* nearly all committed to memory to deal effectively with whatever life might bring my way…thus, it was with a clear mind I harkened back to the thought that *pride goeth before destruction and an haughty spirit before a fall*; whereupon I placed my own pride in a pocket and forged a rapid departure through the cobbled constrictions of narrow streets choked with the huddled masses…and like Lot, I glanced over my left shoulder long enough to make two salient observations upon which ensued first, the query from my colleague as to whether this was where Somerset Maugham the famous writer used to frequent…to which the bar maid replied…*when*…and upon hearing…*sometime around December of 1916*…was answered by a screaming hiss of…*how the fuck old do you think I am?* – while the second was followed by the disappearance of my companion into the bowels of a darkness known only to the ages and in fleeing sorrow to know the name of our fateful end I noticed toward the top of the building a neatly raised plaque rising from the stone façade:

| **1911** |
| **J. T. Silva** |
| **Pantheon** |

Again…at this discovery, I was reminded of the wisdom of *Ecclesiasticus* which admonishes those of the path of righteousness and truth to *be not ignorant of any thing in a great manner or a small*…the pub that Maugham and retinue had made a part of their tour in Honolulu was a shadowy watering hole known as the *Union Saloon* had, through at least two fires, been shabbily reconstructed as *Smith's Union Bar* now sporting a garish plastic sign and shamefully huddled between very old and abandoned brick buildings in a part of Hotel Street that could only be described – even in the best of terms – as seedy and as insignificantly filthy as a wad of gum stuck to the underside of a theatre seat…indeed, I thought to myself.

I remembered when Prince Hal reached his own vanishing point leaving behind his childhood things marked by the slaying of Hotspur, the dying Harry realized this one truth…*that time must have a stop*… and so it did since a full three months had passed since I saw or heard from my former fellow-explorer whom I must admit from some reason had disconnected himself from any communication to such an extent that any news came only as either hearsay, gossip, innuendo, or anecdotal flummery – none of which began to satisfy the keen interest and curiosity that had begun to swell…yet, in the same queer manner through which those visitors who stole away with them the relic souvenirs from their visit to the volcanoes seemed to visit upon this same friend now fading as quickly as rainfall in sunlight…whereupon various issues and strange behaviors began to rise up about him, stories bordering on the tightrope of adventure and demise all of it like a gathering storm of swirling leaves tossed about and littering the landscape to such a seeming critical extent that almost without notice, he had gone away – the only vestige left behind…a treasured copy of a first-edition biography of Maugham for which the notion of irony hung heavily in the tropical air…along with the tinkling laughter of native girls swaying in their grass skirts, a native band paying a lilting tune along the beach, and all this amid the fragrant smell of the *jacaranda*…and still the constant ebb and flow of the Pacific that he found *as inconstant and uncertain like the soul of a man*…but ever to remain lighthearted, debonair, jaunty, and breezy while keeping at least one foot firmly planted within the here and the now.

Mechanical Engineering

There are, or as I recall, or were at one time in a young man's life when the benchmarks
Are as important as normal growth rates, surviving acne, getting the letterman's jacket, scoring
The key summer job oh yes…you are wondering about the virginity thing as well, or prom where
Some fool, a flask tucked neatly in a pocket, announced your engagement.

There are, as I recall, or were at one time in a young man's life when the millstones were
Neither mills nor stones but simple issues inexorably connected in some way to cars, and pride
Of dragging the main as cool as any guy too stereotyped in movies from the 1950's featuring
Souped up cars and girls with large hips, and their faces painted as sinfully seductive redheads.

There are, or as I recall, or were at one time in a young man's life when triumphs were
Measured by the bull nose molding, dished chrome rims, lake pipes, dual carbs, and the
Tuck and roll, and the show-time display of non-pretentious *I'm so bad I'm good I hope*,
Silently slunk down behind a wheel made of chrome chain wordlessly gesturing to girls.

There are, or as I recall, or were at one time in a young man's life when the real *Elysian*
Fields of *Bert's Wrecking Yard* located on ten acres at a gritty edge of town where lay the
Repository of every relic needed to refurbish one's car pushing grimy singles and corrupt
Change over a greasy counter glimpsing the calendar lady as naked as God had made her.

There are, or as I recall, or were at one time in a young man's life to what might be seen
In maturity as simple and vacant the wonderful journey through row upon row of heaps
Their bounty seen in the keen eye for one "possessed" by the viral infection of car mania
Seeking artifacts and uncovering by luck the holiest of holies, the elusive windshield visor.

There are, or as I recall, or were at one time in a young man's life, events where the true
Landmarks of our time stood as clear as science, *A and W Root Beer* was the definitive four star
Gourmet grotto, *Monte Vista Drive-In* was the highest rated visitor destination,
And the *El Camino Real* ethereally lit like a Baptist window was literally the epic king's pathway.

So, here is how it breaks down…I got my letterman's jacket with all the little attachments
Of the flying shoes, the brass baseball, the star patches, and the girls whose names I never knew
Who came around like so many tawdry flies to spilled sugar and in whose only salvation
Lay their vision of success and hopes and dreams resembling remoras on a random shark.

And that was what it was like in those heady days of the *Everly Brothers, Buddy Holly,*
The *Beach Boys* and then our epiphany for many by fire into Viet Nam, to descend into a
Shadowy darkness of the *Animals, Dylan, Hendrix,* the *Dead* and perhaps that says it all,
There are, or as I recall, or were at one time in a young man's life, the inevitable changes.

New Year's Eve

One aspect of growing older… another way of phrasing cheating fate and desperation…

Is in the realizing of what such an occasion as New Year's Eve brings to an individual;
It is a re-awakening of either the hopes of triumph and courage of will over a sea of peril;
A dark mass over which a litany of black chant re-visits the human failings common to all.

If we would look to the anthropologist to view how the cultural trappings define this event;
They would introduce a parade of customs and rituals each a special hallmark of the moment;
About which the genesis and symbolic meaning have faded like the dust of forgotten memories
Leaning miserably against a backdrop of historical irrelevance and uncharted changes.

Or, should one query the scientist of the mind to somehow fathom the elements of celebration;
Or peer deeply to ask "what does this mean" unable to articulate this night as it usually is…
With one notable exception…preserved in the sense by Charles Lamb's deeply sad reckonings
Which pause to remember a love lost or hopes unmet…the ways in which so much has passed.

No time to spend on failure, abstracted joy, or incomplete desires empty as playground dreams;
As woefully unfulfilled as the virgin bride in an arranged marriage of convenience.
So, it is that simple and so contrived to provide a created "progression" and transmitting;
To shed away from the old and venture into the new…innocence all over and once again…

Perhaps to gloss over, re-create, or bury the dead dry specters that haunt the present...

And occupy an uncomfortable lingering a new space that prays for hope and opportunity,

Where it settles like dust on an unused piece of furniture marked with lazy finger doodles

Forgotten to the ages...of young and old the same, like a crazy uncle in an upstairs room.

Columbia – Puowaina

Strife

Let there be no strife, I pray thee, between thee and me...
for we be brethren.
The Old Testament, Book of Genesis, 13:8

Behold the Gardens of Allah
Gesetz zur Beseitigung der Not bon Volk und Reich
Hard to Believe Times (2011)
Kabul – July, 2006
The Cowboy's Lament
Zoot Suit Serenade

Behold the Gardens of Allah

Allah-u Akbar...Allah-u Akbar...
And deep in the bosom of earth lies Abdul-Alim...servant of the omniscient one,
Who sought martyrdom and the destruction of others to become *ageratina altissima*
Where his mother bent like an old twig, mute and brittle shall know him as *snakewood.*

Ash-hadu al-la Ilaha ill Allah...Ash-hadu al-la Ilaha ill Allah...
And scattered within the dry clay dirt lies Bashir...the bringer of glad tidings...
Whose devotion to *jihad* and the ruin of many brought him to become *bidens frondosa*
While his widow, tired and worn like a beggar's cloak shall know him as *devil's bootjack.*

Ash-hadu anna Muhammadan rasulullah...Ash-hadu anna Muhammadan rasulullah...
Buried near the ancient fields of moving hillocks restless lies Fudail... the excellent one...
His testament to the laying waste of children ascending him to become *iva axillaris*
As his family, frail and weeping like babes shall know him hereafter as *poverty weed.*

Hayya 'ala-saleah... Hayya 'ala-saleah...
Somewhere under the marshy sand and withered roots lies Muhtadi... the rightly guided...
That brought death and ruin to those assembled in prayer elevating him as *panicum capillare*
While his friends in shame and humility will know him now and forever as *witches' hair.*

Hayya 'ala 'l-faleah...Hayya 'ala 'l-faleah...
Below the sands that shift like waves upon the seas lies Nasir al Din...protector of the faith...
His legacy of buried souls whose remains are known to God and name him *calystygea sepium*
For those who knew him in grief and unbearable shame will know him now as *devil's guts.*

Allah-u Akbar...Allah-u Akbar...
Beneath a scatter of dead dried leaves that gather without purpose lies Lutfi...kind and gentle...
Who did murder without conscience those in slumber and rest, we praise him as *emex spinosa*
Where they who knew and loved him now bowed in terror will know him as the *devil's thorn.*

La Ilaha ill Allah... La Ilaha ill Allah...
In restless slumber below the destruction of lives and souls lies Imad al Din...pillar of the faith...
Embraced in foul and sickened memory of wanton sinfulness and delusion stays *linaria vulgari*
Who there will forever in grief and boundless sorrow shall know him hence as *Jacob's ladder.*

Agnus Dei qui tollis peccata mundi...Miserere nobis...Dona nobis pacem...
Lamb of God who takes away the sins of the world, have mercy on us and grant us peace.

Behold the Gardens of Allah...where lie the wages of war and perversion of faith;
Behold the Gardens of Allah...there grow the seeds of wrath and vengeance and hate;
You felt secure in your wickedness and said, 'No one sees me,' your wisdom and knowledge,
They have deluded you; for you have said in your heart 'I am, and there is no one besides me.'

Gesetz zur Beseitigung der Not von Volk und Reich

Ein Argument hörte am Bahnhof in Berlin, March 1933

(Law to Remedy the Distress of the People and the Reich: an argument overheard at a train station – March, 1933)

Narrative borrowed from *The Testament of Dr. Mabuse:* Norbert Jacques.

On a crisp morning while standing on the station platform I happened, as might be the case, to not intentionally overhear two gentlemen whom I surmised as such based upon the style of their wardrobe, speech, and demeanor…three factors which in themselves might not be conclusive.

As I listened, I began to sense around me not the Wintery distractions of the smell of bright rain, nor glistening flowers dewy and damp, or the young girls with their gay and lilting laughter so reminiscent of sleigh bells and the nascent foreshadowing of a fresh new year with all its hopes.

None, do I honestly believe, knows he is a witness to history until that moment is impressed upon either him or on the world; and even then, there is little in the way of fanfare or recollection that heralds the beginning of terrible change as swift, as sweeping, and as dark as the soul of evil.

Each owned his distinct articulations as the Commissioner, as was heard to be addressed, poked the air in a frantic mimicry of some *maestro* conducting *Die Valkyüre* while his counterpart who growled and pumped his fists in pure angst as if at sea and drowning was known as Herr Doctor.

And thus began their conversation...

Commissioner: *And this corpse is definitely identified as Dr. Mabuse? There's no doubt of that?*

Doctor: *Unfortunately not Inspector. Unfortunately it's all too certain that this dead man here is Dr. Mabuse...or was.*

Com: *Alas, this assessment of the deceased – is smoking permitted here?*

Doc: *Yes.*

Com: *Seems to me to be slightly, let's say – do you smoke?*

Doc: *No thanks.*

Com: *Let's say slightly exaggerated. In the case of Dr. Mabuse we're not dealing with a human being of value but with an evil criminal who only escaped the gallows by entering an insane asylum. One less insane criminal in the world.*

Doc: *Silence! You have no idea. No one has any idea what kind of phenomenal, superhuman mind has come to an end with Dr. Mabuse's death. This mind would have laid waste to our whole rotten world, which is long overdue for destruction. This godless world, devoid of justice and compassion consisting only of selfishness, cruelty, and hatred. This mind would have destroyed mankind, which itself knows only destruction and extermination, and which could only have been saved in its final hour through terror and horror.*

Com: *Mabuse the criminal?*

Doc: *Mabuse the genius! His intellectual legacy would have turned your world with its police protection on its head!*

Com: *His legacy? You speak of Mabuse's legacy?*

Doc: *No. Yes. Of course not a testament in the accepted sense of the word. Just some of his notes, of interest only to physicians and men of science.*

Com: *I'm afraid Professor, that you underestimate the number of subjects in which I take an interest.*

And thus ended their conversation...

By now the sky crackled with faint thunder far off in the distance measured and unseemly like a heavy presage of human strife, a thick pall settling over the landscape while the movements and emotions became suddenly joyless and everything took on a *gravitas* of peril and uncertainty.

The world seemed to be changing in that instant as I stood on the platform of the train station waiting for my own destiny along the iron pathway once a metaphor of assuredness in life and where one would travel toward new adventures and the unbridled excitement of a free will.

But now all changed and that irrevocably distant freedom instilled and enjoyed for so long might end in tragic consequence of two men and their argument along the platform of the train station as I see headlines that have become the printed epitaphs of this emerging environment of wrath.

I by the tracks hearing the words *laid waste to our whole rotten world ...this godless world, devoid of justice and compassion consisting only of selfishness, cruelty, and hatred. This mind would have destroyed mankind, which itself knows only destruction and extermination,* I fear.

These prophetic words played out in their plainly unimportant sequence of an insignificant event not meant for others nor intended... it would appear...for any other purpose of portent or gravity and thus are nothing more than an argument overheard at a train station in Berlin in March, 1933.

Hard to Believe Times (2011)

There are few surprises in the world today since mass media has become the twenty-first century's *Octopus*. It would be a glorious boon if such broad and accessible dissemination were borne of the highest aspiration and accomplishment of humankind such as art or music or dance, but of course, these cost time and money and talent.

In a strange sort of *Maslovian* world, even the people who inhabit what was once called *first world* countries are now relegated to crafting together some kind of alien existence more strange that those sad, poignant photos of victims, those displaced persons who lost everything, from the *depression* famously taken and archived by Dorothea Lange.

As my grandparents, my parents, and I...all of us grew up on "the American Dream" as that phrase was so curiously coined by James Truslow Adams and has now evolved into an iconic vision as physically and philosophically ephemeral and intangible as the gold dust at Sutter's Mill blinding bleared and drunk eyes but that too was another illusion.

And like my grandparents, and parents, I have lived through the horrid disillusion of the so-called dream interrupted by wars and all the ugly heirs that are the various social, economic, and political shifts; yet, I was one of the very lucky individuals who by fate, or chance, or by incredible will has seemed to have survived at least enough to continue

A life spent teaching, and that with some reasonable material and spiritual success. I will insist if not for myself then to others that I have been lucky to be able to navigate so many difficult passages upon which much smarter and more clever friends, associates, and those unknown to me have foundered so badly for far less excuses.

What becomes of any person for any reason or cause might find themselves at the lowest point described as barely able to succeed at meeting physiological needs and the meanest socio-economic terms that show little human feeling or empathy that would emanate from the milk of human kindness, the charity Christ spoke of so often?

Given these social incordialities, one cannot blame any soul whose lone and base desire is to continue living that he or she might resort to the only ways that connect to survival. What never changes regarding what we term the conditions of poverty of self and soul, is the inevitable and ultimate demise of "the American Dream" if indeed it ever was.

Kabul – July, 2006

A boy sits on the steps of his school house…no longer there;
His head down as dejected as the dreams once held in books
That now litter the ground like the broken artifacts of a culture
Older than the ages and hardly started to repair itself once again.

The winds sweep across the deserts and through the mountains;
But who can protect the children from the fires that rain from without?
The fate of the innocent lies in ashes disassembled, unidentifiable, lost;
Hopelessly and forever made a part of an unknown environment.

In my own hopes and dreams that have come apart, a part of the new;
To change the latitudes, currents, and seas that were a charted path in youth;
Have now and endlessly become a landscape of inevitability without solace;
To course my prayers and my dreams and what I strove for in life to be;

Now nothing more than the weeping in the twilight of another day of ruin,
And the empty and desolate promise of a beginning that will never dawn.

The Cowboy's Lament

To the tune of Garryowen

They say some people are wicked in their ways,
Can't ever know for sure;
Until we pass along some days,
And find out who's been pure.

Now, I've tried real hard to live my life
I've known all kinds of gals;
But every time I try to love
Each one becomes my pal!

They're always in my dreams I see,
The lassies they are with me;
But I can't deny that I do cry
For the girls I've left behind me.

It's funny how some men relate
To issues that enter into their life;
When making choices that are real,
They always end in strife.

I've been with almost every kind of gal
Across the seven seas;
I've seen them all both fat and tall – and everything in between,
The one I remember best I know was the one who brought me to my
knees.

What was it I saw in her that made me think romance,
Not drink nor dry nor tropical heat were any affect on me;
Only that thought that I loved her so through chance,
Struck me such that I'd go so far and blinded I would be.

The toughest times I ever met, were not in danger seen,
Most were often lived in moments I thought were rare;
But life will deal a vicious hand where peril is viewed as real;
And love's pursuit and happiness were never truly mine to share.

I've filled my pipe and drunk my pint, my middy, and my schooner;
My life's been good as so it should, but time is moving on;
Done some things I now regret and wish I'd done them sooner,
While I look back and shift my tack to follow the setting sun.

I've slogged across the swamps of rice and crossed the fields in
Nam,
But this lady on Highway One gave birth as we marched along;
I screamed at her to stop and stay until we cleared her,
But she gave birth for what it's worth and that is what was wrong.

We look at life in many ways, and most of which are real,
But the things I've seen are so obscene that they can't make me
feel;
The problem lies within the core to what end we're here and why,
Until we have learned that we are lost and totaled up to die.

That is the way life deals it out, it's never really fair,
We struggle all our day to learn but they're no answers mate;
Just once it would be nice to see if free will could be free,
But such is not the case in life since we must live by fate.

I guess that's all I've got to say there's little more to write,
There've been good times and rough ones too, I'm ready for a rest;
Living off memories and wistful dreams at night,
Where quiet days I'll sit in ease and enjoy life to its best.

Here's to joy and hope in life, that lives in friends and drink,
I'll rest by shore or sail the sea, I'll hike along trails as free,
The glory of life is hard to find, until we settle as best we think;
In our dreams as children of our mind we will thrive as good can
be;

My steps along the banks of life are measured not in gold,
They are weighed in currency of worth;
And the loving remembrance to the days of old,
For the times that we regaled ourselves those moments spent in mirth.

Now sing the chorus with pride and prayer and thank God for all the fun,
As journeys carry us all through hardships and rough fight;
Back upon those places I have seen and the things that I have done;
I know in heart that peace will be mine by the time and setting of my light.

Zoot Suit Serenade

I'm just struttin' on down the street
My khaki cuffs are slappin' at my feet
I got a *Dobbs Temptation* leaning back on my head
And Olivera Street is where I keep a bed.

My dance steps were learned in a cabbage field
As I gathered a crop to increase your yield,
While you sat lazy near a big date tree
Sweating from the heat and figuring my fee.

As I see things, you owe much more
Since the work I do rots me to the core;
My soul is dead and my dignity is beat
Which might explain why I shuffle my feet.

The brown backs always bent down low
Where every season you try to run the show,
And old men stoop for a meager wage;
Yet, you refuse to see our growing rage.

You insult my *raza* and enslave us all
While we still gather and plot your fall;
You ravage our women and punish each child
By forcing a labor where the weak are exiled.

This song will remind you about your greed
That you have perpetuated as your personal creed;
Does it matter to you where I was born
As a reason why you show such scorn?

We are really no different than any of you;
Our dreams are the same and just as strong too;
You brand names on us that compare us to soil
And you see that your wealth will soar with our toil.

My serenade frees me to glide across the floor
Rising above toward a fresh new shore;
You buy and sell us and treat us like chattel
And think we obey your rules the same as cattle.

You stole our land as my father has told me
And beaten our souls so we can not be free;
We will prevail through the strength of our blood
And you will see the land flow red as the mud.

This dance has begun and will not soon cease
Until our brothers and sisters are living in peace.
Mock us our duty while you still have command;
We will return to our native soil to reclaim our land.

The music is over and our dance is nearly done
While you write new laws enforced with your gun;
But we will strive to live our dream of hope
Our children will grow strong to develop and cope.

So ends the zoot suit serenade for today,
We are united in our faith and so we pray
When we will return to the land we call our home
The land of our fathers as our history's poem.

One final thought about the clothes that we wear,
You have fractioned us as people you cannot bear;
Regard this as our uniform and the anthem we sing
You see us as slaves with you as make-believe king.

You labeled us harshly as *pachuco* and *cholo*
Yet, you are to us nothing more than a *gavacho*;
Your sickened face is smeared with ignorance
And hate cripples your body through arrogance.

So the next time you see me, remember this song;
Think about how your old prejudices are wrong;
Remember our people and why you cannot let us fade;
We will always be immortal in our zoot suit serenade.

HMS Bounty – Makapu'u

Dreams

Very old are we men;
Our dreams are tales
Told in dim Eden
By Eve's nightingales;
We wake and whisper awhile,
But, the day gone by,
Silence and sleep like fields
Of amaranth lie.
Walter de la Mare (1873-1956)

Amo, Amas, Amat
Fantasie
The Land of Sleep
My Small Boat
Swashbuckler

Amo, Amas, Amat

There once was a special time I remember that I spent my youth
staring at girls,
Yes all of them and at once and forever because I was young and
always seeking
That illusory thing called love or whatever abstract and imaginative
terms suited.

As a child whose sleep was as deep as the ocean and as silent as the
prayers of the
Trappists who in their daily toil and orisons did manifest that one
true quality of
Faith and abiding love upon the value and valence attributed to what
some call hope.

Very little in our lives slips through as anything but a piece of the
great puzzle of life;
The ultimate mysterious, opaque, curious, and oddly estranged
fragments that gather
Like dust in a forgotten corner as those pieces which when uncovered
might convene.

Some significant nexus of reality to come together as if by magic
there is sense here
And in this world being made from the mere unrecognizable motes
that is not a part of
The main as noted by Donne's curiosity regarding life and death and
man and nature.

Somewhere in this land there must be a door not simply that as
defined in normal terms
But metaphorical, symbolic, and spiritual ways all combined as one
soaring across its own
Arc of divinity upon a power of hope where these engines were the
twin stars of childhood.

I have many encumbrances in my time; yet, that I have tried so hard to live free of the human
Clutter that builds as litter in the streets; no home where they are addressed; here is a shameful
Act that I admonished a homeless and wretched fool who dared to sleep under a public bench.

I kicking cruelly at his private marker of a discarded carpet soaked in a mutual storm of nature's
Winter rains along with his own personal ruin of urine, sweat, dissolution of spirit, body, and
Soul all wandering down a gravitational pull of the gutter with the reek of psychological death.

To me, he had abdicated control over his destiny and sensibility; his existence in this case lay as
The root of his destruction as he mumbled weakly had been caused by his house burning down,
A phrase so dissolute that it was most likely a recollection of a story told to him at another time.

To one and all, he was beneath any Maslovian order or hierarchy having given in to any number
Of issues or acts requiring succor in alcohol, drugs, or other senseless escapes each inducing a
Bleary and shaded dream that by now maybe never existed nor ever would since all was garbage.

Now, here is precisely what I have wondered about as to what turns out to be these many months
Which have begun to translate themselves into seasons as if one were actually talking casually
About such things as the Spring ball, the Fall parade, the celebrations of Winter and Christmas.

Might he be coming to visit for the high season and such but no…he was a derelict piece of
Flotsam resting as fitful as a sinner and nothing more with no redemption in his pockets for he
Had none, no purchase in his morality and no aspiration derived from his broken moral compass.

What disgusts and disturbs most is the idea of *"omnia vincit amor"* – it does not really – because
The soul has grown worthless, the flesh is not just weak but vile, the spirit is seen as foul, that
Dreams have become as common and as corrupt as a coal quay whore, spent like life on wastrels.

So my beliefs in brotherhood, and charity, and goodness, and inviting those nurturing aspects, of
Human endowments to those in need are now – to me and most of the consumers who feed from
The trough of self-satisfaction – we now serve ourselves the worst masters of our own existence!

I love, you love, he, she, it loves – what a glorious *Latinate* declension and one of the greatest
Justifications of why I had always asked why I am studying this language – but as ever and
Always and firmly was I assured that understanding language was itself a passport to knowledge.

Like wishes and dreams, these are not a part of the real world and never can be, they are a wan,
Indescribable desire of our unconscious self, a child of the imagination of who we should be of
Our dream that we will somehow survive and enjoy this intangible and all too short jaunt of life.

Fantasie

One thing that is certain about beauty is that you don't need to be educated, mature, experienced, or even jaded to think he knows what he likes or thinks he does.

They run the gamut in every imaginable context from who you are, where you're at, and how you feel – like the difference between sitting in a dirty booth in a cheap swill joint on Howard Street or at the *Orpheum* watching *Swan Lake*.

Do you do a ride with *maryjane* or sail on the white cloud...or is your world floating in the water of the heath and heather...nuzzling cigarette butts like food and looking around as if waiting to be rescued or arrested.

There is an endless cornucopia of natural and man-made solutions to stimulate the most feeble of the species where any dream or nightmare can be made into some tangible realty for the weakest and most endangered runts of civilized society who can creep or crawl away from dignity.

How many ways are there to get oneself into another dimension or reason that promote even the strongest to give in to the illusion of escape that usually holds itself out as a new dream of hope wispy and flitting like smoke and ashes.

I like to favor a thought where the characters have concrete descriptions that signal everything about them – their conceit, their habits, their hates, and the nature of the evil that is buried deep within them...so far interred that they themselves are not so self-aware.

They are the usual stock characters who slithered in and out of every dime novel of the 1930's or made their greasy mark upon a wash of films *noir*, hovering in rain wet alleys off Mason Street and lurking in the yawning shadows of Telegraph Hill.

You will see them hunched like old negro slaves, their blackened faces reflections of disuse and bodies so weak from idleness one must wonder what forces could impel them to the vagrant and weedy lot of Stanyan Street.

Some will say with underscored pride "I served my country" in some vague conflict which by now has melted its history into the same fog that begins as regular before the day in the "avenues of the Sunset District."

All of these things – people or places or events – blur as simply as ice melts in an unattended glass, and no one really cares to listen to the story which, after all, is the only thing that gives life to these entities.

Who among the world's population should come forward and like some Jesus among the rabble spend energy and time raising these souls from the dead but there is the catch – they are not dead in the proper way of leaving in a blessed fashion.

Curious – yes – how life can be so deceitful in one hand offering so much hope and intrigue; yet, in the other absolutely nothing...no purchase, no accomplishment, not worth looking back on that which might offer a reason for living.

If anyone ever gave a thought to the concoctions of energies and permutations of existences that have come to the social surface of borderline nativities over the centuries, these sins are the roots of their rotten genesis and human frailty that eagerly consume them.

The Land of Sleep

It is one of my fondest recollections, especially as a young child; thus, I shall never forget
A book given to me by my sister whom I have always hoped and wondered whether she
Had truly understood precisely how much of a significant effect her gift of *A Child's*
Garden of Verses might have upon my life's journey with its random breezes that filled
My sails, the unseen shoals that foundered me, the swells of following sea that continued
To impel me on a sometimes predictable yet often perilous trek full of wonder and awe.

At such an early time, I saw so quick and clear how as a young lad, Stevenson transported
Himself – from the confines of childhood frailty in body only because it is providential that
His own spirit soared – and I as well as other youthful sojourners along discursive paths of
Strange places, of the unexplored land as we the innocent gathered as children in our foreign
Clothing meant for climates and histories unknown to us, our sunburned faces, eyes like tiny
Slits, noses like coral buttons, we shared our youth as a part of a meandering stream of destiny.

The most difficult to perceive and imagine was of course that little world of nod which we as
Children did not comprehend to convert it into the nearly incomprehensible in our zest of young
Adulthood that especially as we careened along upon new ventures while visiting those foreign
Lands, through books, or navigating the seas, encompassing and embracing all the new footpaths

Of education and raw experience, the unique commingling with world events and always offered
The necessary fear and elation with a subtle nodding of triumph in having survived each conflict.

So…it may be here where the genesis of dreams is discovered, its roots buried deep in the rich
Soil of lived life with all its perils and its joys, where perhaps in actual repose a kind of idle and mildly entrotopic state we are indeed fertile in our imaginings, our galactic travels and travails,
Our greatest flights of every vision, real or imagined, to some state where everything is possible
In this ethereal, unscientific, and completely illusory atmosphere we begin the poet noting our
Dreams grew into responsibilities *for the world's more full of weeping than you can understand.*

Dreams and the very act of dreaming are as old and as mysterious as the writings of the Chinese
Poet who captured realities for the drunkard Chunyu Fen in his lessons learned in a deep sleep
Under a very old locust tree where it served as the repository of a mythic land so poignant in life
As in love it bore the same pains and miseries as the waking moments where one is challenged at
Every turn, and events become dares, where living becomes surviving both in the here and now
And as much in the hereafter as the chapters continue unceasing in our imaginations and dreams.

As I grow older, my dreams have become an indistinct series of seemingly unrelated episodes,
Woven erratically as bad tapestry of failed recollection or damaged memory or ruined imagining
Connected only by the backdrop – either some familiarity with recognizable buildings or iconic landmarks –captured so often in postal cards or photographs taken at vacation as indistinct and as unattached as those shadowy memories which surface now and again

in the reveries visited in a sleep so bifurcated by growing age and apprehension that sleep hardly seems worthy of its name.

This might be, then, the reason why poets in their later years avoid the road that follows dreams
Or hope, or desire…all the trappings of the yet to be, unfulfilled youth and its adventures that
Await the eager traveler who in such passion and desire asks little of anything that the world may
Offer and nothing at all of the opportunities and glorious dangers which dot that unchartered and
Enticingly fearful landscape that like the temptations of Christ in the wilderness reach out to the
Starving heart, the unsatisfied hunger and lust of youth heedlessly clawing with reckless desires.

Here, I will stop at these musings particularly on dreaming which for me and at this point has
Begun to stray far wide and away from the inventive, adventurous, and airily exciting forays into
The whimsical jaunts I once visited in the sleep that only the innocent might enjoy…so now to
Reclaim, to rejoin, and to again appreciate those earlier visits to the *land of nod*, I will go as one
Who now journeys for pleasure and ease, with no plan or design, as one who has learned to love
Life, with all its apparatus despite the intersecting roads of strife, pain, disappointment, and loss.

My Small Boat

All of us have a dream or perhaps a wish yet I cannot understand whether this is an illusion that only boys can have or if girls do share the common thought but not just only this minor issue or insignificant component of the ideas and expectation I am certain we share in common though our zeal may be tempered by our gender and circumstance still, I wonder if girls dream of sailing upon the deep green swells or long to see the sails fill with wind, or feel the push and pull in spirit those elemental sprites that compel the voyage.

The journey of adventure always filled over-brimming with the intensity of poets and the concert of great composers whose own visions have charted those same dangerous shoals and mysterious climes or if when one should happen upon the brown earth of landfall which is at once inhabited by humankind and yet then to he who makes the encounter because of ignorance.

Their beauty is derived from that adventure which must never, ever be guaranteed as especially safe or at least mentioned in whisper or charge that from which one will always emerge whole in either body or in spirit or any deal recompensed as insurance or reimbursement from which there can evolve no adventure.

There is a precisely unique cachet that can be attached to sailing upon the silken sea with its promises of adventure, intrigue, danger, and at minimum, a thousand or more delights that eclipse the ripest imagination whether fueled by the ardor of youth or the spirit of overweening ambition or both which in our case may be called stupidity.

Yes, there is little doubt that there exists without the dreamy opiate haze of curiosity fumbling in its shadowy imaginings of a world of sin, or darkness of lacquered walls swelling with fat, supple, green jade figures and the smoky sotto voce of gamblers and whores all plying their trade in the underworld just beneath the sidewalk of say… San Francisco's Jackson or Clay Streets.

The little boat navigates herself well among the stills and swells as if one with her environment; yet, still she carries that captain who is only a reflection of a chapter of any novel he has read about men and the sea and the torments of life he must encounter and he knows, at each step, will be another failure as inevitably chronicled better as an adventure like a marker on a chart or an unseen reef upon a harbor.

As a young child walking with my father at night in Chinatown, I remember how parts of the sidewalk glistened with an opalescent glow of dull light that came through circles of glass ornately embedded in neat patterns on each segment of the walkway and through which one could discern the vague and shadowy figures moving busily about in subterranean caverns that were the human root cellar of the City.

So my little boat will take me along the course that is set on the sea by the wind and the wave and the dreams that compel one to sail along on a journey unknown to places which live in the heart of the dreamer who lives for adventure and there is the heart of it all if all fits together somehow glued loosely by the elusive magic of curiosity and the mystical craving for life.

Old poets called it the lure of the siren sea, where brave men plied oar and sailed across vast spans of blue deeps, where we are told rocks moved and the fantastic menagerie of creatures both human and animal did visit upon and challenge any mortal who would dare to sail forth upon those same uncharted waters.

There is, at least to me, a magnificence of any man's attempt at navigation on land or water and all the attendant fears that must accompany that particular journey; yet, it must be that the effort will be made in spite of every single logical notion that lends itself against both time and tide and that is its unique appeal to both heart and soul.

And here the wise man – Coleridge's land-bound wedding guest, his own life miserably confined to four walls, the squeal of children, the nagging wife, grown fat and unseemly, life all dimming in the end – here taps his chest and asks why venture out with no set plan nor compass near nor map to guide no sextant or chart or phrase that pulls one toward the dream.

Ah...the nature of dreams which are the most unique visions of our destinies so pure and supremely separated from the material constructs of man's social, political, economic, and philosophic meanderings but owe both their genesis and authority from what might be the very essence of that one entity that has confounded mankind for eternity – the energy of one's soul.

Swashbuckler

One of the strangest languages I have ever struggled with yet even now is English; whether it is British or American or the grainy immigrant *gaglish*, I learned as I was developing from infant to child to youth in a family that excelled in Armenian, Turkish, and French, all of whom were the flotsam of a *diaspora*.

My personal journey was epic by any proportion or by an account and by any reason; yet, my acquisition of English was rough with strife of buccaneers or those who ply their particular trade among the violent forests of industrial savagery or in the midst of the violence of those who work an unforgiving land as Quixotic as the tasks of brave Ulysses who muddled his way back to a knitting spouse of whom *Madame De Farge* could be the greatest student.

If handicaps were nickels, I would have been rich enough at youth to buy men's souls or the favor of the armada of nuns under whose well regulated militia sought to correct – and by any means – all the evils unto which these poor innocents could suffer in a bad ear, awkward poise, language barriers, and God-forefend the curse of left-handedness – a clarion signal of evil and the mark of Cain

Early one must ask them "what do words mean?" and do they have any special energy that might possibly serve as an engine of power or an agent of change, or is language simply another way in which those in power hold sway over those whose innocence owes only to a gentle heart, an uncorrupt mind, and no physical treasures such as coin or land or authority or other transient wealth.

There's purchase in that the young scoundrel learns – no wastrel he at such an early age to see profit in language and words so that he might gobble up words as the horse to oats, or owl to vermin for that is how unseemly the coinage is attached to language acquisition as valued and viewed by those whose mantle is the surplice and the black raiment of cleric legislature steeped in dead Latin phrases, rote penmanship, the rule of the yardstick, and the wheeze of *McGuffey's Readers*.

So the question comes full circle asking – nay begging – what does it mean to become or rise above the various stages of personhood or however those who manage civilization – ill-named – mark, denote, or quantify the boundaries and the measurements – most likely to earliest be viewed as medals and later – one can only hope – through achievement they who would aspire and they who would deserve to become a part of the main.

Although it was written and in some perverted way commanded that ownership of one man over another should somehow be in accord with some "god's" will, I know not how; nor, can the most lucid, knowledgeable, and articulate of us argue and sway that this or that is reasonable or good or vile or virtuous, or horrid or noble or fraught with all the dangers precipitate on the threshold of education.

And so like a great frigate should we hope to fill our sails with good wind and following sea – the collective dream that we or one shall at some time ascend freely and by our own will to those plains which we so richly deserve should we strive in union and equality to one and another with respect should thus derive this treasure so long hidden as that was buried by edict or by force, or by church, or by some impertinent law written by stale pretenders.

As in the end the word serves me well at least in the early stage of my life…a blustering, fighting, swaggering, braggart…until those traits were slapped out of me in the many arenas of reality; the squalor of ignorance, the stupidity of death, and the failure of the human spirit have, like the difficult passage, reminded me to hold to myself the values I trust and the choices I make while standing on the balance some share of charity.

Of all the virtues, options, choices, needs, desires, and aspirations that the merest and meekest of the human soul and what might actually define for some "life lived" and for others "self-actualization" – the most important asset is to my mind freedom – and this I define as living each day, each moment and each experience to exercise my options of healthy indulgence – to drink in nature, to stimulate the mind, and to discover ways in which to challenge my abilities and realize my talents.

In my own "summing up" I expect that my path holds a world as delightful and fantastic as the musings in *A Child's Garden of Verses* where travel whether as voyage in time or of mind opens the deeper hidden gifts as fraught with the same angst of doubt paired with the hoped-for joy of discovery – that mirrored in epic of Virgil, Homer, Dante, and yes even the blind visionary Milton who mourned a paradise lost; yet, life is to me prevailing over those false temptations that goad and sneer in the face of one's triumphs whether insignificant or grand or simply precious to one's own satisfaction.

A philosophical conundrum...which of these two is *primus inter pares*...fate or free will? And many have asked if not aloud to their own hearts "how will I die" and nothing has ever adequately satisfied that lonesome query and most have relegated their answers to the dream of dying in one's sleep or by, as if luck would grant as such, "while having sex" but even that begs to wonder why such a strange end to such an otherwise superior beginning like dying from eating, or laughing, or simply breathing – and as such – in a sense dying from life which makes no sense at all unless one would succumb to a self-imposed nihilism or, as could be expected, that astigmatic vision of existentialism or simple stupidity commoner these days as never before.

Considering all the possible calamities that may visit both earth and man, there is little doubt that among these scourges the agony of *Gilgamesh*, the pains of *Samson Agonistes*, the trials of *Moses*, and the issues which confronted *Jesus*...it all ends up the same with a generalization or proclamation in either some dead language or whatever the slang of the contemporary day or mood of any disbelieving people who hate and doubt and wish to destroy what they do not understand; and that is precisely what I have met today and will forever recollect as foul and unwholesome...what many have referred to as Megiddo yet fail to see it manifest in the very souls who presently are among the populous.

In this, the final chapter, it is still most unfortunate that our world is inhabited by those pretenders and self-absorbed sellouts whose only mission seems to be drawn solely toward degrading the things in life most of us who are, or do consider ourselves to be, as reasonable; yet, that is at the very heart of this curious and problematic query as to why and what is behind the motivation that drives or impels ordinary souls to commit such deviant and cruel behavior...and I must conclude that this is what lies at the core of their strange mission which is just another phase in their life's drive which is motivated by the heretic policies of stupidity, amorality, greed, and ignorance of self-awareness and sense of place.

"Skippy" – San Joaquin Valley

Youth

I remember my youth and the feeling that will never come back any more – the feeling that I could last forever, outlast the sea, the earth, and all men; the deceitful feeling that lures us on to perils, to love, to vain effort – to death; the triumphant conviction of strength, the heat of life in the handful of dust, that glow in the heart that with every year grows dim, grows cold, grows small, and expires – and expires, too soon, too soon – before life itself.
Youth (1898): Joseph Conrad, 1857-1924)

Five O Five O Street
Formative Youth
When I Was a Kid: Reflections on Growing Up
When I Was Six and School Was Fun

Five O Five O Street

A long time ago, there was an almost photographic recollection of a little kid in corduroy
Trousers and a colorful striped tee-shirt that had horizontal lines - and he played gleefully...
What the philosophers call pensive, what the scientists call acquisitive, or what the honest might
Call childhood if such a time could be allowed to rise above the ordure of violent memories.

There was a place in heart whose nexus lay the intersection of Santa Clara Avenue and O Street
Populated then by good people who were the last of their generation – the survivors of so many
Social, political, economic, religious, and ethnic issues – weighed, measured, and gauged both
By the valences of ethnic calipers and rejected as well on slides as much as any lab specimen.

Five O Five was that generation's Ellis Island, a sort of clearing house and in its own unique way
A rite of passage, a breeding ground, and, one can only hope, a beginning, a start, a launch, a
Prayer , a spark that ignited a long forgotten past filled with so much memory of those dreams Extinguished by misplaced aggression of delusional power of nationalism, pride, and genocide.

Over the years and times that have passed, one prays that temporal passage might hope to teach
That the days of recollecting are not forgotten or forsaken but in some tangible force taken to
Heart where at such as Five O Five of hope and grief of remembrance and of worship, of prayer
And of solace, of desire and of dreams that we are all children living in the light of redemption.

The real beauty of Five O Five lay mostly in its idealized, endemic features – etched and eidetic

Of the old Victorian, its fence of lilacs, the yard so ripe, the barn with its musty memories past,

Tomatoes fatter than Aunty Moorkoor, onions as fulsome as old Garabed, a tender sweetness of

Soft loquats as sensual as Araxi, or the pomegranate's sweet fragrance reminiscent of antiquity.

How do we define heritage if we should still believe we have one; is there an historical record

Written or handed along as lore uttered across the tongues of elders to the children who could

Hope to own and reclaim – if such were possible –their history, a legacy, a culture, and the truth

Whatever that may reveal; but it must be uncovered: all explored, illuminated, and understood.

We are not done, the children, the survivors, those who remember, those who cannot forget –

Nor will we forget; there will always and forever be a legacy etched in human toil – not written

Or passed along by oral history – but always and inexorably through the living and all those who

Have struggled with the angst of tradition and distanced morality of cold and ancient wars.

They and we who have existed wearily down paths of joyless pain, suffering and sorrow, always

And at one's back pressed darkly in one's mind all the old hatreds and wished for vengeance;

To change such violent and useless anger that by sheer will cause it to bud, blossom, and bloom In places such as Five O Five amid the cluster of lilacs, bougainvilleas, honeybees, and children.

Formative Youth

Here's the true story…as well as I recall, specious but please indulge me;
My brother-in-law was in fact a kind of pivotal character in my life,
Older, smarter, wiser, and more clever having sailed his own uncharted rivers,
To take himself to places as Coleridge and Byron recollected, and I was young at seventeen.

He was, he claimed, the heir of the first "white' child born on the *Mayflower*, Peregrine…
What might if by chance or coincidence a black, cinnamon, crimson or yellow seed had been;
Somehow nefariously as if by secret path or plan preceded this so-called auspicious occasion,
Appearing out of the unknown sea like some long drifting coconut seeking permanence.

But that is moot as I recall since much of what one thinks one is… is merely stuff.
He, of whom I speak, held great sway over me a blank slate…the mind as white paper;
He nudged or intimated what steps I might and must take in my education now beginning;
Though I was committed to the Jesuits by my father's will, but that was of little concern.

The matter at hand was "experiencing" in the real world whatever that meant…he noted;
And he was never clear since the term could never be a component of a Catholic education;
Which I will admit was not real in itself looking back upon endless Saturdays in redemption;
Chanting the long-forgotten creeds of Nicene, the acts of contrition and kneeling endlessly.

A remarkable journey through the ink of Miller, Nin, and all the artists we were warned against;
Of Joyce, Camus, Kazantzakis, and Durrell; of Amis and Pound; Lawrence, Sartre, and Flaubert;
In a wayfarer's library, grey walls, hard benches, posters that boasted of America's heartland.
All of Savonarola's vanities bound up together in the wire kiosks of the Greyhound bus depot.

And somewhere near Crete, or Clichy, by Maroussi or Taormina, with Maugham and Haxton,
Straining to imagine what Lawrence saw in Frieda or what compelled Harry and Gustav to kill…
"Aim at the chauffeur, got him!" in this odd venue of laughter that resolves the ills of the world;
Shape personal meaning of life, of love, of loss, and the journey into unknown deserts we hear:

*Horridas nostrae mentis purga tenebras, accende lumen sensibus?**
Purge the horrible darknesses of our mind, light a light for our senses!

Medieval Prayer

When I was a Kid: Reflections on Growing Up

What frames a person, makes a youth a beginning, the habits of life
that shape and sway
Which mark or motivate and somehow set the course that may be
what we will or would
Or could become from our experiences and views and dreams and
the hands that compel
With or without our knowledge that they are aspects and forces of
the chemistry of youth.

My course was marked by eras of significance as borne out by
historical bench markers
And the cast of characters who....for better or for worse...populated
that weary plane;
Where in carefree summers we would wander freely and without any
set contingencies
Upon our own device that in every sense freed us from the bolted
rows of desks of school.

The earliest friendship was Norman, my cousin, who like me
measured time in the country;
Time spent in visits to the smokehouse filled with slabs of meat as
ancient as the Old Testament;
The drying sheds ripe with the figs of Smyrna, dates curing as they
did when nomads traveled,
All as envisioned as in the past as if in preparation for an arduous
journey upon the Silk Road.

One could trace the sentiment of childhood of breakfasts far early
before the sunrise began...
Over strong black coffee, detailed with swirling goat's milk, of
wrinkled Kalamata olives,
The homemade "farmers" cheese soft...like thick pudding...and
sheets of unleavened bread;
We ate as serenely as Jesus...humble and pleased that we wanted of
nothing but our freedom.

The paths of childhood carried the ever-looming backdrop of the Armenian Apostolic Church,
Air thick with the incense timeless as the myrrh carried by Balthazar, the chorus of old women
Always shrouded in black no matter the circumstance whether good or ill, the bearded priest
Whose constant admonitions were *be good, honor your mother and father,* and *eat all your food.*

Dotted along the emerging vistas were the strange names untranslatable, mystical, impenetrable,
Enigmatic as the patience of Job or the soul of man, where here was Hovsep, there was Aghavni,
Hysmig…the jasmine flower…and Antranig whose particular *cachet* carried the forlorn label,
A sad little kid who was the iconic reminder of the Diaspora and multitudes of starving people.

All was antiquity and not just through a child's eyes; we grew up in the fields of our fathers…
Among and between the rows of gyp corn, driving the Allis-Chalmers tractor or resetting discs;
Adding weight to increase depth…opening the sluice for the irrigation…making little rivers;
Taking in the noonday heat…the sand-like soil running through tiny fingers and wondering.

Pretending to act the grown man and minding the Mexicans occupied with the grape harvest;
And secretly laughing with them and learning how to slap the floury dough into tortillas;
Or to engineer the corn husk and tamales while navigating the perplexing cultural crossroads
Which irrevocably separated us from them…the landowners and the migrant workers.

We evolved we boys from killing bugs with magnifying glasses or songbirds with bb guns...
It might have been a natural evolution toward maturity and conscience or a process learned
By rote and drill day in and day out at Saint Theresa's based on values, what some call ethics;
And yet we emerged as boys still...but older or what some have called mature and learnéd.

We had not reached social standards because when I called my sister something bad in Turkish,
My father would drive me by the city water works, a large windowless building where I was told
As assured through his authority...that this was the final repository of boys who behaved badly;
From whence there was no exit; and that the lessons in catechism should serve as ample warning.

Yet, perhaps by luck or some other mystical fate or an assured future through *orare et laborare*;
We were blessed with Uncle Aram, a man whose graciousness, generosity, and sense of justice
Have been chronicled elsewhere...a man who understood the stray and alien hungers of youth;
And had taken such a difficult journey himself to save his own family so many years before.

Who was a part of our jaunts and flights of risk and folly, and, as if by some ancient secret mark
He might leave that we could recognize but to all who would during desperate times of hunger
Should gather in the fields of summer in Turlock, Yettem, Dinuba, across the San Joaquin Valley
And leave for us the last of the melons, luscious as the breasts of virgins, full of a promised joy.

A pale quiescence of a Persian or quaint blush of the Honeydew, the bright allure of the Casaba;
For we boys who sat in the near barren fields of the afternoon sun, our grime spattered hands,
Soot masked faces from the depot watching with fascination the engines trailing innumerable
Box cars, flat cars with exotic names on their sides heading to or coming from faraway places.

As we rested eating our melons, the juices dripping as careless as a Summer rain down our arms,
With the sweet knowledge that only boys can know and appreciate and before the day was ended
We would bathe in the ice cold waters of the Delta Mendota secure in the hope that life would…
That life could…always be as clear and cool, and as joyful as these reflections of growing up.

When I Was Six and School Was Fun

I will forever have in my memories of school embedded mostly in dreaming of a world outside
The greatly anticipated field trip to – for example – the *Oscar Mayer Weiner* factory where we,
Like little maggots, consumed with alien vigor the five inch tubes our own fingers in harm's way
Some mystery meat that we watched emerging from stainless steel vats like so much pig iron.

I remember the bliss at the altar of Mary of the day we spent at *Sunbeam Bakery* inhaling aromas
Where we were encouraged to hedonistically grab at the staff of life as it rolled so hot and fresh,
Tearing at the cellophane shaping with our little hands the beautifully soft, refulgent white bread
And being smacked by Sister Lavinia as we dared contort the dough as it was the body of Christ.

I can be thankful that where we grew up as children there was a rustic country dairy as primitive
As the Eleusinian mysteries while secretly dark as any Masonic Lodge and shrouded in murmurs
Were people toiling in regularity of labor somehow and some way slightly strange to America,
In a language as exotic to our ears and as foreign as their faces in work at the *Danish Creamery.*

I recall the excitement of the industry and the constant yelling of the foreman in steady cadence
With the cannery's mechanical clatter, endless conveyor belts moving the harvest along the path
The occasional failure of the assembly line whether human or mechanical, culling the produce,
Fruit not quite perfect, somehow blemished, taken off the road of life, tossed aside like a refugee.

Yet, I think I over-analyze nearly every aspect of all the *petite choses* of my entire existence,
And this process of habit must be life's way of notifying me my days of youth and innocence,
A glorious wonder at the food we eat, have now been relegated to objective scrutiny at market
Losing the magical labyrinthine twists and human toil that transfigured the earth to such bounty.

So here I will stop to give important pause to the self-realization that no matter what one's age,
No matter what one's stage, no matter what one's phase…should one forever treasure and value
As family, the labor of the human spirit, the transformation of the soul, the riches of the land,
And oh…those wondrous journeys and discoveries I made when I was six and school was fun.

Sacred Heart Church – Punahou

Religion

All good moral philosophy is but the handmaid to religion.
Advancement and Learning, 11, xxii.14, Francis Bacon (1561-1626)

Metamorphosis: Religion and Social Justice
The Confessional
A Confusion of Tongues: Modern Media
The Curious Transformation of Heroes

Metamorphosis: Religion and Social Justice

One of my most glorious memories swelled in a true eddy of angst in that I was young, in college, in Vietnam, returned to the real world, changed with more focus, more fear, and a little more principle...such are the changes that befall us in times of peril.

How did I nourish my newly discovered growth – by rebelling against the very corruption that poisoned the lives of youth, that destroyed my friends who had years ahead of them, that lied and corrupted its own power to sway an entire swath of children to, at one swipe, ruin their lives and in so doing, make them the agents of death against other youth in other places...the shame bears a stink worse than ordure and a mark far more sinful than that of evil itself.

In my newly changed life...and it was that exactly almost ironically like the rolling away of the stone and yet another baptism I emerged not much older but certainly wiser...to take my place in the protests that so famously marked a truly remarkable era of contrasts, of anger, of love, of change, and of a hope for change.

I remember the marches as they were called through the prominent streets of San Francisco always on seemingly crisp and sunny days that held out hope but in reality we little understood the issues but somehow were articulate enough or more likely fired with an energy that must necessarily well up in the hearts and minds of anyone who has ever felt the sting of oppression and so I, like so many like me... found ourselves walking and carrying signs, singing and yes even praying that somehow change would come not by the enigmatic hand of God, but curiously, I considered, by the hand of ordinary men.

Religion is a very tricky construct which relies a great deal on ritual, artifacts, legends, lies, an incredible history of existences, and a revolting number of followers – and, of that group fall into place many sorts which I allow might simply be divided by consequence of station, psychology, intellect, socio-economic status, or random placement – but, all have one salient flaw in common; and that is the belief whether firm or fleeting that from cause comes effect; and denying the sciences of physics or biology, must substitute as the ultimate arbiter in those events beyond our ken and it is this, I point to, as the inane and childish heart of those who hope against hope and fail to take account of their own actions whether as purposeful as an old China hand who plots along the rugged coasts to the puling child lost in the mire of his own muddied world of confusion.

Behold the taxonomy of those revelers who in their way claim to have found salvation, or hope, Jesus or Jehovah, the talisman or the planets in our sky – all the same, one and all but each person celebrates in his own style – the Christian who attends church when advantage calls as in holidays, another so-called Christian who gambols with venomous snakes, other Christians who wear black and spend their last days in darkness weeping audibly over the passing of someone unknown to them, the Hassidic Jew whom no one understands, the Reform Jew who does not understand himself, the self-loathing Jew who like Greta Garbo wants to be left alone, the Muslim whose life is now a sequence of events led in the shadows, the Muslim who is newly converted because he has tried every other religion, or he has nothing to hold out as hope in life, or he has spent years in tier three at the *State Penitentiary* doing twenty-five to life.

And there are the Buddhists so simple and private that this belief must seem to most, as nothing more than a state of mind ranging from those who celebrate holidays at shrines, answering to the sound of gongs, clapping their hands, and attempting to live normal lives in a modified type of serenity, where there are those who don gray robes and wander among the living in society as if they were alien creatures who are tolerated by virtue of the fact that they seem self-sufficient – yet, observe their brethren dressed in saffron robes with their shaved heads, their eyes unlit, their minds removed from the world at large who make meaning when dousing themselves with gasoline and ritually set themselves afire while sitting perfectly still in a lotus position, eyes closed, palms open and raised upward like a reclining statue of *Kuan Yin* – posed, postured, serene and so it goes with an almost circus like procession of humankind, all dressed in their costumes and acting out in their own foolish way – what may be called a kind of ritualistic dance that in some arcane way provides these participants some kind of succor or a moment of solace, away from a chaotic, uneasy, and oftentimes confusing reality to bridge over to a place that can only be determined and defined by the inhabitants of that particular world that is not connected by the wires of history, or socialization, or fear, or consequence…the very things that compel people to act irrationally and impel them toward religion.

Other aberrations have become a part of this strange fabric and were there time enough and inclination, the seeming unending list of true believers could fill the most ancient of valley, but that is not the point because what I find intriguing is how in contemporary times, people continue to create ways to pervert their logic and dilute their beliefs through various chapters of life which I can actually reflect upon as point of interest in my own time which reveal just how obtuse understanding of belief and how tenuous one's relationship to any deity really is as manifested through the actions of young men drafted to serve in unjust wars and how they chose to have their dog tags read Buddhist as their religious designation as if this curious *shibboleth* were a kind of code for please do me no harm as I am one of you my brother.

I suppose in their youth and ignorance they must have believed that Vietnamese were, somehow universally Buddhist and that might transfer some kind of mercy upon these young white fodder, in the hope of being spared; yet, in my own personal experience, Buddhism had very little to do with the ugly relegations of that war and that I also knew first-hand that the Viet Cong cared less for redemption and more for body count, as did their American counterparts both for whom might stupidly claim that God is on their side, but that is an empty prayer because in that environment, God is simply not there; and when one finally accepts that unassailable fact, only then and perhaps forever will he come face to face with his own moral self and the culminating acceptance that religion – or belief in it – will never assure upon any plane of existence that one will survive…which is precisely why war and death are arrogantly and euphemistically referred to as the sacrifice upon the altar of freedom.

126

The Confessional

This may be one of those stories that is impossible to believe let
alone imagine as it is written;
Born of the spiritual beliefs instilled in those who would follow the
dictates of religious canon;
It is true nonetheless and what makes it incredibly special is its
very impossibility and pathos.

Imagine if you can an ornate wooden structure and here you should
choose the wood;
A rich brown but browner and darker because of age and incense
and the ten thousand
Breaths and sorrows upon which it has been visited over these
many centuries past.

Consider it as ornate as a sepulcher or tomb, a repository wherein
lie the unholiest utterances;
Sotto voce, mumbled, rasping, halting, and embarrassed tones, *sans*
embellishment no inflection,
As somber as the grave, as menacing as an imagination filled with
apocalyptic visions of mass.

For the sedative purpose of temporality, envision it as bi-
chambered…two rooms four by four
Eight feet high, one with a short bench uncomfortable; the other
with only a kneeler as hard as
Old age and disappointment, unforgiving as self-pity and rancorous
hate brought by the church.

Oh the stories or exaggeration these walls might reveal somehow
through deep layers of lacquer
Of thick slabs of polish meant to maintain the *spiritu sancti* like a
private communication device
To some god on high, staff of cherubs sitting idly by to take your
personal contritions for mercy.

Such is the genius or innovation in this pseudo-philosophical
condition of human fear and dread;
A supplantation of the "oracle" but this venue for the common
penitent in all of us holding hope;
Who purchase into this mystery, those so afraid, so subservient, so
pliant, so ignorant and weak.

What man would now review the parade of sycophants who in their
unique ways dance the ritual
Down their own private *viale dei dolore* on knees, flagellation, self-
abuse, humiliation, shame;
Their pitiful suffering is a bitter prelude to their own death march
palling heavily with the dirge.

It would be pleasant to imagine one individual priest who for
reasons unmentionable here would
Record and catalogue these utterances of sinfulness with the same
holy, delicately detailed, mind
Or devotional righteous hand as guided *Beda Venerabilis* in whose
eyes was history so narrated.

I might wander into a marble-vaulted repository and be seen
viewed like a hungry tourist eager,
Wondering at the meandering journeys into the imagined depths of
personal fears created for us;
Made manifest by the *agnus dei* who have dutifully visited these
valleys of despair before me.

A Confusion of Tongues: Modern Media

In the long ago past...a millennia ago at least were the scribes, a special order unto themselves
Sometimes priests or other genus of self-aggrandized, pseudo-anointed hierarchy of specialists
Whose domain and dominion lay sway over all events human whose words were made legacy.

In principio erat verbum, et verbum erat cum dei, et Dei erat verbum.

Across the evolutionary trail, the messages began to gather their own unique momentum;
As a long awaited affirmation being heralded, or an expectation fulfilled in one's dreams
And dashed against the shoals of reality to founder on some distant, shadowy, and vacant reef.

In lui era la vita e la vita era la luce degli uomini.

Humankind has a constant irrevocable and inborn need to regenerate and feed off the *word*;
Synthesized into the genres of music, poetry, narrative; yet, unlike other evolutionary steps
There are no natural barriers, no selective processes to filter out the slag and dross and effluvia.

Como una voce di uno che grida nel deserto; preparare un wa per il Lord, fare il suo percorso rettilineo.

There is notes St. Cyril, a dragon by the side of the road as corrupt and foul as the nature of man
Who puts himself before God and all else, as he writes his own history full with indulgences and
Self-importance marked by the cancer of vanity, distortion, and a corruption of perceived power.

Un diluvio di parole non è mai senza colpa, chi controlla le labbra è saggio.

Like scribes and prophets of yore did as their progeny climb that same metaphorical tower;
As at Babel did dig deep into the well of their own narratives marking them as critic, arbiter,
Speaker of some truth on high and he who divines the new world by their own coined phrase.

La lingua degli uomini retti è d'argento puro, il cuore degli empi è di valore temporaneo.

So disposed are the legions of pundits in raiment of religious, political, and social perversion;
Their light fading slowly…dying…extinguished as the canary's breath in a cave of darkness.
Forever lost as written on the wind or carved in snow or etched on the sands of a distant shore.

I profeti profetizzano falsamente e lo Stato orso sacerdote con i loro mezzi, e la mia gente ama avere così, e cosa farà alla fine della stessa?

I would leave the scribes, shun the false prophets and avoid forever those who would claim truth
As their own; still, in their withering moments like an old moth dying in the dull and fading light
Of a vague and far off glow shall wither, crumble, and collapse to their inevitable dust and ruin.

Così la volontà di Dio e il maledetto destino dell'uomo.

The Curious Transformation of Heroes

In nomine Patris, et Filii, et Spiritu Sancti.

The life blood of the classic tradition most often finds its particular aortic connection in a mixture of strange, inexplicable deeds or events followed by an equally unbelievable set of moments usually witnessed by so-called adherents who feel either through empathy or desire or simplistic symbiosis a need to connect to something greater than themselves or at least a feeling or desire that transcend the ordinary within a less than extraordinary existence.

Among the pantheon of figures larger than life emerged from two sources – and here is where actual genesis is in question; for there is little to deny the power of the *saeclorem* of black robed priests with long wispy beards, sporting two foot mitres and draped with a rosary whose beads are larger than fists, and about the neck and shoulders wearing as if deigned by the gods on high as from some warrior's victory a gold crucifix the worth of a large, prosperous kingdom.

There were other icons of course because that is precisely the exact nature of growing up in a family as Catholic as mine and as illustriously fabled for the dual mechanisms of survival and assimilation – we turn to the word – *in pricipio erat verbum* – to include the commandments handed down we learn to Moses from God on high – and *primus inter pares* deciding as an unschooled child between the particular list in honoring thy father and thy mother, or John the Baptist, or Jesus, or Paul, or Joseph, or Mary or simply assuming like all else in this scattered family the need to come together under one large extended clan poking about blindly for answers and some sense...any at all... desperate and dependent as it were...for a direction or sign.

As if to emulate the house of God where the altar is festooned with all of the brass gadgets, the cross, the stained glass depiction of the stations, all of the finery of the struggle between good and evil that has over time and habituation – become the set piece, the trappings, the furnishings, and psychology of tradition and place which have compelled ordinary people to march, to kneel, to chant, to follow lock step rituals so arcane and muddled that they owe their existence as much the same as an orphan would to parents who are unknown – like vagabond trash that flies along as driftless as litter upon a deserted village path.

When one speaks of deities – it does not matter the era, dynasty, or particular belief system; there seems to be one constant element which one refers to as omniscient – at least for me – that omniscience lay in the properties of voice and frequency, by the power of regular and well-modulated stories, narrated in dramatic fashion, crafted by the competent hands of inspired artists, transmitted with complete and uninterrupted power as if, by master spinners of tales from on high – which in my young and naïve childhood was derived in Hollywood in studios where imaginative souls let their thought float as freely as incense smoke wafts in a zigzag patterns whirled here and across in steady rhythmic motion by stupefied censers who play their role.

That is how the transformation began, as ascended from super heroes, cowboys, and an interesting array of all kinds of characters evolving from the futuristic forum that might chance – if such could be possible – be the body of literature so old and rich that none would dare to challenge; but such is the nature of man's incessant quest of those elements and essential qualities that make life a thing of beauty, or of remembrance and respect, or of a kind of coming of age and learning from our mistakes, of epic journeys and travels to fight the metaphorical dragons and emerge as those who fought the "good fight" to go on and become themselves the teachers, leaders, parents, and heroes of another day in a totally new and different world.

But hold...I have yet to answer or respond in some way to the assertion made at the onset of the curious transformation of heroes which has been evolving for many years at the same time both slowly and quickly as if it were some alien invasion bent on taking control of the earth's population and as seemingly mindless and without any foreseeable plan or divine intent...more like slow moving lava or glacial ice incrementally covering vast expanses that no one seems to take note of nor for that matter care; but, it moves forward unchanging and unchallenged, embraced at every turn gathering in its wake the true believers who have either willfully or without thought given over their once cherished values, their long held beliefs, and their intrinsic nature and ability to make the charitable choices in life as these effect themselves as others.

I am a firsthand witness to this egregious transformation and it is only because I find myself more pre-occupied in the present world of books and art and dance and music and all the other beautiful, vaunted endeavors of humankind that I have been able to isolate myself from the temptations of becoming a part – an infinitesimally small and mitigated part – of what some now call social media, although that epithet will soon show itself to be a greater irony than any can imagine as these sheep buy into wholesale and at any cost the links that are generating a population of soul-less individuals unable to think independently, or fend for themselves, or work and live within the very components that used to make up the fascination and reality of human nature and their shared caring and consequences of humanity.

They are walking around as if barely awake, in a state of pure entropy constantly connected to their new gods of electronics and media fog that is a constant and unremitting hovering of weather neither good nor bad but stable to maintain just enough atmosphere to the legions of those connected to their ipods, ipads, iphones, cell phones, laptops, twitters, emails, voicemails all surrounded by a twenty-four hour cycle of unending media that ranges from so-called news reporting to ersatz entertainment, to make-believe self-help programs, to the absolutely bizarre and abstract anomalies that human nature can produce out of some strange and foreign design all in the name of mass communication which in itself lies at the heart of this conundrum.

No longer are individuals allowed, let alone encouraged, to think on their own, for themselves, to create their own beliefs and fantasies or delve into the mysteries and problems associated with making difficult choices, nor to set aside time for the needs of others, or for much needed introspection, or self-awareness; rather, the emerging generations, mewling and puking in their own special style, are reliant upon instant gratifications which are as reliable as the specious accuracy of entries into Wikipedia and endure as long as a Reno wedding, and where these connected souls find themselves feeding on a life of constant bargaining over everything in that their most extensive needs – no matter whether earned or deserved – might not be met.

This is the crisis of the short-lived and soon to be completed future which surely will end in an ocean of self-serving fury and monumental struggle over competing selfish material needs built on falsely inflated egos and an overweening desire to outdo your brother or sister; where all those "of the social network" as they will be called, will see their day not in a lake of fire, but rather in a disappointing and rather dull closing down of systems – a monumental failure based almost solely on the giving in to the personal greed, the misguided pride, the sinful desire to see oneself as above the rest, a steady practicing of hyperbolic hypocrisy only too late to discover forlornly in the end that the prophets were right all along – *to give that thou hast to those in need, and thou shalt find treasure in heaven* – but the transformation of heroes has brought that notion to an irrevocable and tragic end for now and forever.

Aloha Tower Pier 7 – Honolulu Harbor

Places

The Men! O what venerable and reverend creatures did the aged seem! Immortal Cherubims! And young men glittering and sparkling Angels, and maids strange seraphic pieces of life and beauty! Boys and girls tumbling in the street, and playing, were moving jewels. I knew not that they were born or should die; but all things abided eternally as they were in their proper places.
Centuries of Meditation, Cent.iii, 3:Thomas Traherne (1636?-1674)

The Night, the Fog, and the City
Sands and Shoals and the Deep Blue Sea
The Places I Have Been
Young Girl in an *Ao Dai* – Tran Hung Dau, Saigon, 1967

The Night, the Fog, and the City

Sometimes, I wonder what is it that inexorably tugs at me
To vicariously find enjoyment
In *film noir*.

It certainly cannot owe its curiosity in re-living any adventures
Committed in youth since
My life had not yet begun.

What curious elements draw me into that shadowy world of alleys,
Steaming manholes, surging, scurrying yellow taxis and
Tall slender women in furs?

There is an odd and melancholy affinity toward topcoats and
fedoras,
The sleek dark cars that glide through the night with silent ease
Along rained touched streets.

Where could any fascination with modern cities choked with
skyscrapers,
And the wandering grey anonymous people strolling through the
night
Have impossibly found its genesis?

Why would such an environment made up of those characters more
at home among
Hammett and Chandler appeal to my senses to such a degree that I
can easily see the
Headlight glow of furtive men stirring about?

Cigarettes, bright coal lamps, clinging on lips of strangers in
thoroughfares do guide those
I have never met, whom I might like to know, or have the chance to
visit there,
And become a part of them…in the night, the fog, and the City.

Sands and Shoals and the Deep Blue Sea

Let me make this perfectly clear...I love the ocean;
that salty concoction that holds a personal intrigue for me
a connection I feel as natural as one's birthright...
and that is what I will base my love upon.

The earliest recollections were at *Point Joe* where
the big ships foundered and, as a little child,
I played among the reefs and tide pools full of
the genesis of life itself.

Opal Cliffs resplendent with its heights of
land and waves so beautiful that otters enjoyed
those deep blue waters cold and choked with
thick green kelp healthy as a blanket upon the winter surf.

This love of the ocean did not come easy
and as I remember was the same elusive didactic lessons
that were a natural part of my father's playbook which
was historically and notably filled with epic metaphors that
always whispered in some arcane Biblical aspects
a certain *quid pro quo* as he would put me upon his broad shoulders,
wade far into the Pacific, go above his head, and thus impel me to
fend for myself... like an uncertain youth on an uncharted path...
unsure, frightened...and always respectful of an ocean I knew
to be as powerful a force on earth and in heaven as love and
friendship; as faith and as strong as the bonds we could not yet fathom;
simply because we were that young, that innocent, that fresh.

One of the graces of age is patience;
and here, in this poem, I will take pause
to reflect and respond to the tides and turns
of the waters of the earth and the shifts in our nature.

I have read so many books filled with the images of Japanese pearl
divers which I always thought of as never real; but, of course they
are; lithe, lean, and strong Polynesian men standing straight upon the

hard backs of long boards gliding across waves toward the shores, and far distant echoes of men in whale boats their bows tethered to the behemoth they sought to harvest; reedy Chinese fishermen in awkwardly angular craft and square sails floating like pieces of paper upon a sunlit sea that lay so still; and all the rest of humankind plying each their own way through squall and following sea in ships as mighty as any fortress or brave as any dream.

Inspired was I from those devoted individuals
not to dive for pearls nor chase the fish,
nor challenge nature's fate and will;
but to discover what that ocean might to me reveal.

I have no transport but myself to sojourn
as it were to the ocean I have visited
and the waters I have swam…and afraid was
I in strange places that were to me so exotic.

Drawn therefore I suppose by the Lorelei's song
and the siren's chorus that no man can ignore;
yet, to go forward upon some unknown quest,
and that to me is the hero's ultimate journey.

The Places I Have Been

Ah, the lands and people and places I've seen
Fill memories with sights of countries I've been;
Each marked with events especially unique
Up dark murky rivers and shores choked with teak.

I've sailed across the vast azure seas
And touched upon the strange Chinese keys
Which lie in mist and among shrouded hues
To descend through fog and to see such views.

As mushroom dots on a silken plane
Odd landscapes verdant from a constant rain;
Such territories shining like emerald stones
As ancient these are as ancestral bones.

Such are the wonders that one might behold,
Places of mystery of which old books have told;
But there's nothing as wondrous as in that place
Where unfold the stories on a porcelain vase.

Etched on the faces of men in the shrine
Who patiently pray from the dawn of time,
Carts that have rutted the paths and the streets
Paint a legacy of history where the adventurer meets.

Where lies the dreams of a curious young child
Through pictures and words he imagines the wild
Rugged lands, high mountains with terraces of rice,
The sojourner confronts a new kind of spice.

Far and deep in the sensuous climes
I ventured through Siam through curious times,
Where the winds fill the sails and awe one with fear;
The perils abound but no daunt to him of good cheer.

He plies the waters as the birds of the sky
Along the stretching waves and monsoons they fly,
Where the longing for discovery feeds an unbridled joy
As does the wonder of magic could entrance any boy.

Bent women in places like old Viet Nam
Chew betel nut daily to help them stay calm;
The brown glow of teeth like the bronze of old
Transforms their frailty to a dignity so bold.

In Laos I walked through jungle so thick
And encountered such evils that would make one sick;
And continued to pursue along a curious trail
Of the temples, the statues, wild monkeys and travail.

Where by each step is measured with trust
How much might a man be measured by crust?
That must be a part of that aspect of hope
Which carries him forward to seek and to cope.

In Burmese villages whirled young dancing girls
So beautifully dressed with their fingers in curls,
Graceful as swans and their gestures so sure
As ancient these rituals in a drama so pure.

I thought I had dreamt of old Mandalay
Where in sleep I believed I would surely stay;
Half awake with a terrible fever and pain
With gin and quinine held a cure for my strain.

I lay on the floor of an old *nipa* hut,
My reveries floated and my senses were cut
As wondrous images of which children wish
Saw I squadrons and formations of flying fish.

Unconscious I languished on the Indian Ocean
So deeply lulled by its gentle motion;
Blue waters flat with the glow of life,
Smooth seas so calm they bore little strife.

Imagination will take me to a far distant shore
And once again too will open a door
To adventures as windows to the core of my soul
And I pray I don't founder on some distant shoal.

I have sailed to the deserts of old Araby
Where I have been greeted by the winds of the sea
So strange were the camels and figs of the land
On this dreamlike landscape all covered by sand.

On a drunken whim and cold specious leads
I planned an exodus across the sea of reeds
To free myself from Pharaoh's hand
And make my hajj to the Promised Land.

As fortune deemed it so, cooler heads prevailed;
My journey was ended and my quest had failed;
When into my life came fortuitous chance -
A trio of sojourners who seemed locked in a trance.

To the west we shall venture toward far Marrakech
And take along with us this miserable wretch!!
It was I they addressed as they stroked each their beards,
I obediently followed as if compelled by the weirds.

And sadly now as I look back on it all,
I hardly remember these events, I recall
As in joy with age should we thrive on our sorrow
And regard all our time as life that we borrow.

My dreams begin fading with every attempt
To look back to voyages as if they were dreamt -
I will venture again in search of my youth;
Each step as a balance and a legacy of truth.

There can be little joy in saying goodbye
When one has a choice to seek the why
And pursue the strange winds that fill our sail
To discover new lands through the storm and the gale.

Where my purpose for living lies in the sublime
Venturing blindly along a strange time
And to hope to discern all there is one can find
As in heaven's design to nurture the mind.

Before we grow old or unable to roam
Our mysterious plane and fastened to home,
I cannot imagine in time or in place
Never taking the chance of experiences to face;

And look back on a life that so much I do love,
To enjoy in restless waking and dreams as above;
In life and in sleep I will continue to try
Seeking new ground and joyful triumph to cry.

To forever trek toward the dark and the deep
Whether here or now or in dear blesséd sleep,
To venture neither knowing the where or the when,
But recall once again all those places I've been!

Young Girl in an *Ao Dai* – Tran Hung Dau, Saigon, 1967

She was as singularly beautiful and as
Seemingly delicate as a porcelain figure of
A doll – the kind you see encased in a glass
Box in stores in Japan.

You would never meet her of course
In the matter of everyday acquaintances
Or by any chance of luck because you and they
Are so terribly different.

They are archetypes especially heightened
During times where the environment is steeped
In blood and the messier attendances of war
Are such as which confute reality.

Yet, irony cannot be an integral part of this
Particularly extraordinary equation since irony is
A main operative precept of warfare in Viet Nam
Nor can or should one trust any vision.

While waiting patiently at the intersection blurred
By the typical traffic of humanity scurrying to and about,
Random *cyclos*, and the intrusively deadly swath of convoys
Bleating out their horns, sirens, and gunfire;

There she stood, and still as elegant as the finest carved jade,
As ancient as the Ming Dynasty and as delicately beautiful
As Kuan Yin, palm upraised, serene and supple, erect and mild,
With a smile that seemed more enigmatic than *la Gioconda.*

Oh gods that be, have you tricked us once more with an illusion,
Or a dream, or even a wan and fleeting hope born of desire that
We might discern some small vision of beauty, grace,
Tranquility, and love real or idealized?

Therefore, after these seeming long ruminations,
My own personal perspective, the long suppressed moment upon reflection
Whereupon she placed her dainty forefinger against the left side of her nostril
And blew an unceremonious well of fluid from her noble, elegant, and oh so common nose.

"Marnie and Kai" – Sisters

Love

Dear as remembered kisses after death,
And sweet as those by hopeless fancy feign'd
On lips that are for others; deep as love,
Deep as first love, and wild with all regret;
O Death in Life, the days that are no more.
The Princess IV (1847): Alfred, Lord Tennyson
(1809-1892)

A Father's Daughters
Aunt Lila
Kristine Sends an E-mail
Love Is Just Another Four-Letter Word
The Only Love – *Gaudeamus Igitur*
Juvenes Dum Sumus

A Father's Daughters

I am only now beginning to see
Some reason to life and why I am free.

Cecilia Kaiulani and Marnie Kealakekua,
My two daughters whom I have loved forever.

I have long asked myself why might I live
Though an answer came slowly it meant I would give.

Though I am only a father and cannot be what every child
deserves,
I have tried and toiled that I could fulfill your needs.

The most curious thoughts were once tied to my youth,
Through trials and journeys came reasons and truth.

My two daughters whom I have loved so much;
Each of you has gone on a separate path.

Love for so long meant as little to me
As an abstract longing which was never to be.

Each journey, while I watch and hope, I worry;
It is I who has not been what every child deserves.

There are places where love is as cheap as illusion
Where those who seek romance find only delusion.

My fervent prayer is that the spirits of your place of birth
Will guide you safely across the uncertain currents of life;

Thoughts written upon sand owe an ebb to the sea,
Erased my beliefs once held in trust and charity.

Yet, I hope that your course will be straight and true
Because I could not be what every child deserves.

Tsi-Nan-Fu...Tsi-Nan Fu...Tsi-Nan-Fu.

Aunt Lila

Aunt Lila was for me a very rich and textured book of history, manners, and social grace – another world with another view in so many ways different than the dirt rich and sunlit land upon which my father drew every breath…the initial chapters were etched in the earliest photographs which as a child I attempted to mark and measure through the decades in which she made her own cachet upon me.

My childhood visits spent with this grand dame – and yet at my youth – I recognized her as precisely that and deserving of that title as much as if her character were idealized into a narrative as an entry into a dictionary, a thesaurus, or a social register.

At some date in 1918, I saw her married photograph, Uncle Hovagem dressed in his smart military uniform each of them looking as bright and eager to forge their own fortunes as they should dare.

Uncle Hogan, as he assimilated, looked stiff; yet, he always was with a demeanor of a banker who has nearly lost all the wealth of those who placed in him their trust – yet, Aunt Lila…beautiful and as delicate as any flower, as graceful as any ballerina, as elegant as a Hollywood starlet whose fame rests solely in her virtue of nature – yes, that was her to me.

There were two seasons which were a part of my education – I will call it such since there is no one here who can actually verify the reasons for those fortnightly stays with Aunt Lila who to me was always first a tutor in the graces.

Winter always pale in fog and light rain – the three story mansion in Berkeley Hills, gleaming stairways of oak, Persian carpets as thick as the beards of the prophets, the glistening columns white like children's teeth against a verdant green of ivy, and ever the silent, faithful scurry of long-time servants anticipating every need whether real or imagined.

There was Sydney – an immaculate Ethiopian – this I surmised from the collection of *National Geographic* with its serious yellow covers and uniform thickness where they lined several shelves in a special place of the library where I might sit dutifully for hours reading while Aunt Lila attended to her own social duties as writing letters, planning parties, organizing voyages across sunlit seas, and coordinating the elaborate dinners and such that provided entertainments of such genuine grandeur that they would rival the epics of the lavish soirées portrayed in the films of the 1930s and be reviewed by grateful guests or re-lived in the society pages always smart, ever delightful.

Upon the first meeting with Preston the driver – I was too young to understand the title chauffeur – who looked like a soldier of great importance, tall and trim with the bearing of what I imagined could be a captain fearlessly leading by countenance alone a group of frightened souls into battle; he did not speak nor was there any need to do so, his tailored pale lavender outfit, with brass buttons, calf high black leather boots shined and darker than the hearts of evil men, with his lavender cap tilted ever so jauntily back upon his head – full of black shiny hair, and a high and noble brow…but I was young and every man looked to me like a soldier.

There was a photograph, another that signified a different era which as I recall was sometime during the 1930s with Aunt Lila astride a dromedary camel – she pointed out the difference to me as a part of my lessons – where she had spent "some amount of her life lost in the mystical desert of Morocco where time meant nothing and all was consumed with the eternity of vast starry nights and forgotten days…" and she would drift away leaving the room and me sitting cross legged on the floor trying to imagine the rest of her story…I did not, however, ask for any further explanation.

Among my favorite photographs was one taken somewhere in the African continent where Aunt Lila is perfectly outfitted in jodhpurs and boots, a *topee* and a streaming silk neck scarf flowing down her back like a bride's trail – she gripped tightly in her left hand a *Holland and Holland*, her left foot atop what appeared to be the carcass of a very large lion like the one they had at the beginning of the movies – which she assured me when I inquired that she had been, with great prowess, the executioner.

Early during those winter mornings I would be awakened and we would have breakfast in an outdoor area or so it seemed – really a solarium as I learned – where later fortified we would cross the strip of ocean along the Bay Bridge to the City which for me was as fascinating in my mind as say Paris, or Athens, or even Constantinople before the war in those black and white pictures within the covers of the *National Geographic* which was my world outside.

We would step out at Union Square with its canyons of buildings, streets thick with people of purpose, and after the fog, a light rain dewy and then a day as clear as the eyes of a child, as bright as the mind of youth, Aunt Lila holding firm my hand as purposeful as a ship's captain attending the wheel across a vast and heady sea.

Aunt Lila always almost never said anything but of course she did not need to – she led by example, or gesture, or by the sheer will of who she was – and that to me is what is enduring.

In the summer, we went to the hillside villa – for it was that in every sense – perched atop a hill, a sprawling indifferent casual existence ordered only in the sense of Aunt Lila, her photographs, the library, Sydney, and the driver.

The entry was a deception that invited and engaged, its sprawling flagstone patio partially buried into a niche of the back of the mountain and forcing as effect of – upon entering Aunt Lila's house – one was compelled to views directly of the breathtaking vista of the grainy green, brown, and purplish valley far below as befitting a villa perched like a delicate bird on a limb of an ancient tree upon any island in the Aegean, the white washed walls gleaming in the sun, the blue shutters as deep as the waters of the Mediterranean, and the handmade coral red tile formed of native clay from recipes as old as the Mayans, and forged upon the thighs of Mexicans brought to this place specifically for this aim and architectural signature that would often be a part of the conversation at cocktail parties.

By the 1940s, when I actually became a real part of the human landscape, I saw firsthand my earliest accommodations of my education the social graces imbued fortunately among two conditions which favored my particular lot – economic wealth and unrestricted love – all in my own family and within those two cultural artifacts, I was heir.

My young mind was impressionable as in these early heady; years I was the ultimate juggler who by fate was raised in unremitting love from extended family, born of the primitive toil as seen on my life in the groves and vineyards, ensconced in the somewhat gaudy trappings of mansions fitted with spiral staircases which led to large private rooms, where moved steadily the maids and chauffeurs, kitchens as large as playgrounds, and the glory of one's own bedroom.

It may have been that I was somehow blessed, or special or significantly gifted in ways that do not come to individuals until they have had time to pave their existence with mistakes and lessons learned.

If there were a reasonable way to explain the genesis of my earliest beginnings, it would emerge as three elemental conditions – family, education, and fortune.

While family and fortune are relatively easy to comprehend and see how their effects are measured, education was and is a serious enigma which requires a deeper examination.

Education – the beginning – dual accounts by grandmothers Sarah and Marinos who daily recounted history as they knew it from the era of the *Gospel of Saint Matthew*, the days of the caravans, and the times of Tiridates and the conversion of Armenians to Christianity and the holocaust of Kemal Attaturk – but all of that was simply prelude.

For two old women whose lineage could be traced to the Bronze Age, they were very adept at weaving together an interesting tale that implicated the horrific deeds of the "Young Turks" and their own difficult journey toward salvation.

Had I been a little more sophisticated, I would have suspected they were two in cabal but they were nothing more than relic survivors of what as young girls had witnessed at great peril, in their own simple lives and now, I believe, they saw themselves as living time capsules, a sort of distorted narrative of collected nightmares to remind us to never forget.

In early drama, there is always the chorus which either presages the events in the story or echoes the narrative to give it an epic quality and substance and in this case, the chorus was the Armenian Apostolic Church of Saint Paul's, an ancient brick building as old as Methuselah reeking with the smell of incense transported by old Balthazar himself as he did that very night for the Christ child.

Had I known the word or sense, I would have termed the alliance of educators as collusion, but of course I did not – I was young, I was pliable, I was faithful, and I was what I later learned was called having the mind as white paper.

Mathematics has always held an interest to me not out of my enjoyment, nor from some native understanding, but solely from its own ambition of parts which fit together like cogs on a machine that invariably move forward, clearly, with purpose to some incontrovertible end.

There always before me were the sheer numbers and volumes of the one irrefutable fact, the repository of modern knowledge that had become an iconic representation of research, voyage, discovery, and interpretation of the word – and that what lay at the heart of my education regarding history and at that time, but that matters little.

The third component regarding education for me and its image of my own history is just beginning to emerge from an environment and impetus that has been apparently so close in front of me that it was not possible to focus on, let alone recognize, until now and as I step back, does this aspect lend itself to clear recognition and its effect might viewed as such a profound personal life force.

This final aspect can best be defined as an intellectual hunger fueled by curiosity and skepticism – and it is that latter perspective that may have caused me to wait so long to write poetry, find respect in the voices of others, and disdain the blind notion that with power comes respect.

However, such feelings are diversions from the very substantive issues and events, the people, and the places, and the admixture of history and lore painted so inhumanely over the span of time distorted by the twin deformities of politics and religion.

But my visits with Aunt Lila, the forays into those rich and rarified places where one is allowed to enter by status only, were for me as enriching to my development as my father's purposeful decision to enter San Francisco by way of South of Market even though our ultimate destinations were Fort Point and the Palace of the Legion of Honor.

This is precisely what may be the nexus of different worlds in which I found myself from time to time wondering always why I was here and to what consequence if any…?

It seemed to be the collision of such diverse worlds…what makes my life worth examining and – yes – chronicling; so, this is the nature of existence and education with their various goals and how they allow and invite and interpret and how we make meaning of our personal histories.

In Aunt Lila's world, the roads were marked by a strong and demanding assimilation that had a constant and insatiable appetite which fed on the arts, nourished itself by association, amplified its integrated belongingness through performances at the opera, visits to museums, voyages on the *Lurline,* and the development of one's tastes and educated ear for classical music and the demanding efforts in reading and literature.

In my father's world, driving by Third and Howard was a living lesson plan that demonstrated the daily tableau of human misery and the failure of man's spirit, as our car would pass along the streets littered both on sidewalks and gutters with the remains of alcoholics; my father the teacher pointing to the marginalized waste and connecting the cause, the effect, and the consequence for anyone – me – who did not respect life nor himself…his world for me was a real classroom which could set up its virtual desks in any place dictated only by time and context, with lessons so fluid yet perceptive that they might be considered as lofty and deep as the sermons by Jesus whose audience would gather more quickly than attendees for a baseball game – and that in this interpretation has been likened often as a real reflection of the game one engages from day to day, and yes, my father loved baseball the way others embrace the stories in the *Bible.*

In the end, my experiences have become as much self-inflicted as not, which at the heart is most interesting since all this time and at least until now I believed in earnest that I was solely responsible for my own destiny – during times squatting in the middle of recently tilled acreage with my father commanding me to take a handful of soil and understand that this mass of earth is my sole benefactor – a significant and important part of my life as responsible in relationship to my well being as if it were a blood relative.

What a rich and wondrous legacy which I can now appreciate the ways my schooling evolved; the didactic and direct teachings under the tutelage of Aunt Lila in whose hands I was directed along the paths of gentility and high culture, entry into the realms and lives and discourse of worlds filled with the products of art and aspiration – of the goodness and achievement for which we constantly hope and pray will ultimately define civilization.

Happy is the individual who discovers at such a late time in life when so much has passed; yet, of course this is not to deny the likely possibility that there is so much more of that time to live and delight – and this is for the very best part – to know, to understand, and especially to enjoy every event and each non-event no matter the size or the consequence, whether in light of importance or none that the halves of my education – really the vitals that have nurtured me both in body and in spirit which have served me so well.

So it is this I submit in loving thanks to Aunt Lila who in her own way has had such a deep and abiding effect upon my journey of the soul as much as anything – and on the whole, given the circumstance of my curious existence, I owe serious gratitude as well to my father – but he has been graced elsewhere and often in my thoughts in respect for his metaphorical and literal translation of relationships between and among nature and man – and therefore, may it never be said that I have misunderstood or underrated my affiliation and respect for Aunt Lila and the entire cast of humanity which in each his or her own way has made all the difference in my world; and most likely, serve as the reason I teach and pray and have in my heart charity that I might do the same for others – but one can only hope.

Kristine Sends an E-mail

Here is an interesting incident I would like to report, and I do not understand why it happened; I met a lady and we began to converse; she said she wrote poetry and I said I write verse which is not so different with the exception that what I write is closer to prose than to poetry and I wanted so much to be accurate and above all honest – what the faithless scoundrel politicians call transparent – because, after all, entering into any relationship with any woman will always have the seamy trappings of politics and other behaviors associated with manipulation and mistrust.

As if in some ancient ritual, we exchanged business cards which reminded me of the dreadful English novels of the Victorian Era where a gentleman leaves his *bona fides* such as name and address and some such other collection of titles and trivia which are collectively meant as little more than a marker not unlike animals who wish to place their cachet upon a tree. I do not think very deeply on such things because they matter little to me since they have no substance.

Most of what I have seen and experienced of human interaction is either primitive fumbling and extended periods of awkwardness or worse, practiced routines of what has been scripted either in movies or television depictions of what social standards would rate at minimum all the horrific, disloyal, and inane – all of which is relegated to the ninth circle of Dante's *Inferno* set aside for those who would devote their existence to betrayal.

Let me be the first to admit that I may be flawed in two ways – a limited social life and a healthy mistrust of women and that for many reasons. When opportunities arise, I look upon them as the blooming of poppies in a field in their glorious golden glow growing like weeds on unfriendly and unclaimed ground.

Yet, they are as honest as the smallest seed that owes its lot to the breeze and its fortune to the soil and its existence to the elements of wind and water in storm and in calm.

I have gone over the events a few times and have avoided thinking too much about what happened because in the long run, it was not that important to me.

What were my mistakes that caused her after that initial missive with her four clumsy poems – it was ended as clearly as death, irrecoverable and irreconcilable.

My response was honest which is something I perhaps should never again be with anyone borne of a decided need to make serious choices in these delicate days that affect both life and career.

In my own sincere words, I stated frankly that "it did not matter" though it did that I asked her relationship status and as I explained a little lamely that we were "under a microscope".

To be fair, I mentioned I did not understand the meaning of her poems which might have been better articulated by lying with full and unmitigated gusto and thereupon heaping instead rose petals and high adjectives and extremely glorious language of praise and joy upon them but I could not do so because as was my purpose and previously stated belief I sought honesty.

Each poetic piece was pathetically flat with its drifting lines scattered randomly here and there while – I want to make this clear to one and all – where the worst of them was an iteration of *Heloise and Abelard* which I explained was bothersome and very problematic and not a part of where I live which is in what I call the real world of the here and now and free of any pain!

Then, extend those thoughts or apply their sentiments – or project them if you will – into on-going scenarios that might play out if she and I were one and that is just one problem at the core.

If one were to look to reason rather than emotion, then the properties would present themselves more clearly as the facts and these are: she was a mother of two, a wife to one, and in limbo.

Add to this a smoky mixture of vague words and phrases "separated from my husband" which heralds frightening visions of every dime novel and B-movie that relied on the old theme of infidelity and retribution which almost always occurs at that most sacred and profane point in the dewy newness of the relationship where one's vegetable love is about to ply that quaint honour!

I have read just about all the great books – the plays, the epics, the stories, and tales – upon which their very existence is dependent upon this old and familiar theme.

Here is the irony and possibly some sort of resolution for those weak souls who constantly look for closure or some other artifice they have learned to make a part of their co-modified lives.

She will never know why I stopped writing, why I chose to end any kind of uncertain and possibly dangerous relationship especially one that would bear the caption *muy peligroso!*

There is a final sadness in a way to all this and it may sound cynical or satirical and that it might be…but nonetheless, these are the facts and whatever decisions were made by her will always remain unknown to me and will forever make their mark on what can only be tallied as another enigmatic disappointment attached to the histories of women at large as then and even now.

So let the poets write words of praise to love and women and of their breasts and eyes, may the artists exalt their beauty in paint with faint smile and blushing cheek, and it should forever be remembered that all of them will be relegated eventually to either a deserved objectivity or an illusory caricature symbolic of all that they were not nor never could they be. And that is sad.

Love Is Just Another Four-Letter Word

There are few things in this world whether one is talking about concrete or abstract notions or philosophies or feelings as that overused word love which has been thrown around as often as rocks and curses at any congregation that declares itself to be something representational of what human kind aspire either to be or what some would look to portray society in some context that really to me and always is and has been and most likely will often be nothing more than a dissonant and distorted and heavy-handed collection of our deepest flaws.

Love is an abstract term which at birth can invoke nurturing and charity but the world's history is filled with the opposite where we have witnessed hate and massacre and holocaust which have been the chapter headings of every era and that does not really create any surprise to anyone who can survive and live to go beyond the unfortunate ugliness of traditional human history where one will discover that words or terms like love mean very little if the truth be known.

Oh, I have been loved and indeed that quite well and familial love, brotherly love, love of country, love of various women, love of my children, love of friends, love of teachers, love of priests, love of dogs, love of anonymous people in Kenya and other strange places who claim to be solicitor or barrister holding at minimum a million pounds sterling or some other amount which in their words are my good fortune and not sufficient in that recompense which must have its metaphorical and nuanced level in Dante's hell – yet, still I was loved so!

Yet, and please wait and be patient especially those of you who are young and hold hope that *amor omnia vincit* which was written as a sentiment as ancient as graffiti on a wall of a Roman whorehouse, that if fortune shines upon you, that for whatever reason you accidentally fall into a loose and tawdry definition of harmony in a relationship, or as most will find themselves inexorably stuck in a pathetic symbiosis which over time will evolve into the twin evils of legal encumbrances of property and joint custody!

These then will be the emerging issues along with the inevitable and ineluctable eternal imprisonment of mutual infirmities, age related disabling incontinences, and the pathetic death of life and marriage which has as its grand finale as co-dependency and a constant and morose atmosphere of rotting slowly, enabling the poverty of a life lived well, and a constant and steady and droning reminder of the law of asymptotes – so much then, for love, or for marriage, or for any hope of every attaining the good life.

The Only Love - Gaudeamus Igitur Juvenes Dum Sumus

(Let us rejoice therefore while we are young.)

I cannot pretend to be anything but what I am which is comprised in my own assessment by the sum total of my biographical data, my history, and my credentials all of which might paint a complete picture but never can nor should they do so; and let it be known that I understand that there are those parts of my life and time that I cannot, or choose not, to remember with any ardor.

I have spent more of my life as a teacher than I have as a parent which I find somewhat unique in that, as I look back upon the years, I have interacted with more children and have devoted more time and energy to those souls unknown to me in exponentially immeasurable ways than I can fathom though I try because I did have influence yet care little since they are on their own.

But there is a point to all this – and here it is as best as I can imagine; that I have devoted my life as so consumed by that passion and honor that is the realm of saints; but I have and as unerringly knelt at the holy altar of academia repeating solemnly my orisons as lectures, and my personal gospels, and stories of myself which might illuminate understanding in the minds of my students.

It could be that at my earliest age, let us say five or six, exposed shoulder to shoulder or in some other and indefinable way closely connected to the nuns all of whom – they claimed – spoke the word of God, or of Jesus, or at minimum the words of the prophets which actually now in present time make a clear and meaningful sense to me yet never questioned those words from on high.

Hence, the conundrum that embraces at once and consumes the children of the catechism which is re-enforced by the edict of parents, supported by the Catholic Archdiocese, assisted by the educative zeal of young Jesuits and promulgated by the strictures of the old and new testaments, the peculiar *sturm und drang* of everyday life with its horrific disasters of infantile genocide.

But of course, we grow older and again just a little more circumspect and approach a point where we comprehend themes outside the structures of religion and education or their commandments and instead we begin to see them as stepping stones along an unseen path, through gorse, in dark of night, by inclement weather and fears which challenge and divide us from our earnest pursuit.

Let us rejoice therefore and while we are young might have more to say about our lives and deeds in the spirit of inquiry of professors whose expression and desire for youth is well rooted more deeply in the halls of academe where the long-beards daily rejuvenate themselves in the clear water of knowledge where as children we are taught by the poet.

"drink deep, nor taste the Pierian spring; there shallow, draughts intoxicate the brain"

Yet, here the *Bible* warns us all in its curiously dark, deliberate and labyrinthine ways:

"for in much wisdom is much grief: he that increaseth knowledge increaseth sorrow"

Still the chorus sings its praises toward the heavens, for the angels, in a plainchant way:

"Vita nostra brevis est, breve finietur venit mors velociter, rapit nos atrociter nemini parcetur"

Then, it must not seem so unusual that the only love addresses those elements that exist where knowledge and learning are the groves of trees with deep and solid roots fed by the earth that instructs us all through history as we are reminded *"atque inter silvas academi quaerere verum"* and we rejoice – we will be assured our one real love.

Where we, the teachers who for so long have toiled through teaching and learning and creating the worlds and visions for our children, will sing with great zest that sweet chant *"vivat academia – vivant professores"* and blessed am I among that collection of souls who share in the sacred song and fervent prayer where in all labor there is profit.

"Old Man" – Central Union Church

People

Les bourgeois, ce sont les autres.
The bourgeois are other people.
Journal, (January 28, 1890): Jules Renard (1864-1910)

Detestable Things
The Great Poets
Solitude
Thoughts on the Nature of Reading
Tramp Stamp
Uncle Arthur at Lavabo
Yellow Fever

Detestable Things

My first inclination was to write "things I hate" but that single and over-used word is both too abstract and too personal.

It is difficult to recall the seeming endless pile of issues, events, and people which are problematic as well as those who have been bothersome.

Especially disturbing are those movements which stir in the souls of the desperate, the ignorant, or the hopelessly willing an urge to do great and harmful acts against nature and man.

Yet, human history is marked and chronologically catalogued by these sordid and barbaric illustrations of man's basest acts.

Some incidents are as remote as the planets of the solar system; yet, they impact each of us as a pebble tossed into the middle of still water.

Even in my brief and relatively uneventful existence, I cannot help but feel the tug and sway of world events as far away from me as the nether reaches of the arctic or the vast deserts of Asia or Africa but still they touch me.

Nor, is there any pre-context to history or social aggregation in crazy flux – as yesterday, to illustrate my point, when I explained my family was compelled to flee to a freedom held out by America because they were a part of the Diaspora.

I am sickened at every level as this woman whose credentials certified her as an historian – a history teacher her credentials reflect – asks what is the *Diaspora*?

Another woman next to her whispers "...you know...the Jews, Germany, Poland...the holocaust and concentration camps...you know..." she sheep bleats to her friend in a hapless prodding of pointing out an incomprehensible and mindless failure to consider such an epic human evil.

She, that one who has so horribly failed at every level not just of the comprehension of history but of consequence, stabs a slice of *Havarti* unceremoniously with a clear plastic fork and stares at it as if imagining this as a part of important ritual of existence.

Is there an insult so looming that it would never merit rising to the surface given the facts that the human landscape is littered with the dead carcasses of good people and the *ordure* of misspent beliefs and failures in religion, education, and compassion.

Firmly in the grasp of her tongs lies an oily croissant as an assured and agreed element to be consumed without question or meditation that she...of specious knowledge, her personal and professional *credentials* in question, a genuine risk to the education of our greatest assets – our children – she turns to me and asks "...are you a Jew?"

I have often wondered if the social scientists or perhaps those who delve into what must be considered the darkest corners of the mind or of the heart – if each could possibly be separated from one another – and guess, or speculate, or calculate somehow on a graph or some other imagistic format the degrees of shame, the darker aspects of perfidious deeds, to chart somehow the insidious and ugly aspects of man-made plagues, of retaliation, of obliteration, of epic ruination.

I am not a Jew that I know of or that it would even matter to me, or for that fact that I am Armenian, or that should matter since this stupid woman knew so little of history that all of this began to pale...as if somehow nothing really mattered, that life and death and history really held no valence, no importance, no consequence, no matter...history itself relegated like an old uncle locked in an upstairs bedroom, imagining himself Napoleon and taking his meals as they arrived punctually under the door frame.

But real life is much worse than that stale caricature of how we sometimes see ourselves or the ways in which we de-limit the feeble-minded among us whom God or Allah has touched as special...I

171

would gladly elevate the status of those many among us who inhabit a world that some deem crazy and others certify as insane.

Yet, how much more crazily out of touch are, for example, the dead wood among the groves of academe whose only delight is drawn from self promotion, or the priest who hides behind the false currency of piety while taking succor from the touch of young boys, or private indulgences of *Christ's blood* from a small bottle hidden in a brown bag...the politician who rants daily about high values, morality, the weighty issues of personal ethics and all in the name of constituency and guided by the sacred aegis of charity and ...during the night, or rainy afternoon, at unseen moments steals away to construct a bribe, consummate a sinful desire, to break from routine and wallow in the arcane bawdiness of concupiscent behaviors even when smeared by the cheap mascara of fame and charisma...odors and deep stench of sinfulness which cannot be masked by perfume or tailor-made suits or by crafted reputation drawn on a four generation name, or by the meddlesome provenance of a so-called military record of cowardice, curried as bravery for whom so many died to blur forever the true record.

Shamefulness, duplicity, and greed must all hold a special place within the holy taxonomies of ill sworn behavior that are the passports to hell.

I suppose it would be too much to wonder and to be able to see how the putrid stock of liars, cheats, and frauds spend eternity; although by my own admission though, I can neither see nor know, I can imagine these foul destinies and at least hope.

What fatigues my heart and plagues my mind is the ice cold current of fear and certain doubt about the qualities of men which can lead them to act in overarching sinful ways; yet, I am not alone in this confusion of cause...for as Juvenal pondered...*nemo repente fuit turpissimus*...and so it goes.

"No one ever suddenly became depraved."

The Great Poets

I have always wondered what makes a great poet, although I suppose living during the earliest civilizations, the candidates were relegated to a miraculous few who could read and write and somehow had enough leisure time to spend in what some might call idleness while others would frame it as contemplative meditation or some other such posturing as if legitimacy were a requisite component to greatness.

I can hear them now, the twenty or so odd lot of white men mumbling in their scholarly accents as cheap and phony as a sideshow freak, rubbing their hands, shaking their wrinkled heads, collectively stroking their gray beards and asking what does this young pup show for credentials, where are his *letters of transit*, how the iconic W.W. Norton & Company of New York and London elevate him into our vaunted pantheon of long dead and ill remembered artists whose dull and mute existences were eclipsed by their writing which is always typically less exciting than their real lives painted with the dreary stuff of tabloid news.

If I were more suspicious and less intellectually curious, I might be compelled to draw lines between the tragic circumstances which seem to hover over the odd times of this group of artists and the drama they produced and inevitably I would begin to wonder which came first – the pain or the pleasure, although I must admit that it can be a little difficult discerning true feelings from the parlor tricks played out on paper by the complex charades of a disturbed mind and convoluted psyche.

What is it that makes a poet – is it an era, an age, social consequence, political or religious strictures, dysfunctional families, bad personal choices, uncontrollable habits, or simply the abundance of incurable psychoses that seem to be drawn to the fragile of mind and spirit like ants to a picnic or maggots to dying flesh and those two not so unrelated to one another given the ordinary circumstances that are the typical architectural landscape of those who write poetry – who are of a common thread so thin and transparent that none are sufficiently aware of their own mental delicacy nor the intricately unusual turns that seem to be an inherent part of a predictable journey which in so many ways is the culmination of a self-willed prophecy as if at rainbow's end, there is a peaceful resolution in one's musings.

But there never is that ardent wish for serenity as if by words alone one might visit and settle somehow, I know not how, into that lush glade of tranquility and be free of the bonds of life that like so many endemic, thoroughly overwhelming, crippling, unforgiving, viral, incurable angst and leave as their own trademark the deeply etched marker of deservedness by an all too inviting host – like the reef to the sea creatures or the skies to the planets, or as natural *as flies to wanton boys are we to the gods; they kill us for their sport...*so dies the poet in a pool of stupid banality.

Here we open the book that lists the great poets, we choose at random as does the "great spinner" that Hardy referred to in his "Convergence of the Twain" that somehow is a proper fit for the histories herein yet never revealed: Elizabeth Barrett Browning, a gloomy reflection of her corrupted lungs and failed heart, a set of conditions exacerbated by her palliative use of opiates and leaving behind an unsmiling face where in death she might *answer to the ceaseless wail of the Sphinx of our humanity, expounding agony into renovation* – but that will have to wait.

Here lies another great poet: consumed by depression and marital separation, a tortured and unfulfilled life scripted in poetry, wandering thoughts about a father she suspected of war crimes, a pregnancy which she alluded to as a journey as hopeless as a descent into hell, a steady diet of anti-depressants, and the wonderful finality of sticking one's head in an oven, turning on the gas, and moving on to that great unknown – what a strangely uncomfortable and untoward means of leaving this world and shuffling off this mortal coil.

Is that John Donne I see...once a student, a Dean, a member of parliament, a member of the clergy, a doubting Catholic, a womanizer, a squandering philanderer, a host who carried myriad illnesses through his squalid existence until the end he committed himself

174

once again to religious fervor like a death row inmate who finds God and – at the final moments before the moment – rejects the inevitability of death and he, dying penniless and unpublished until his passing, only to be metaphorically resurrected and remembered in the tombs of *anthologiā*.

Why who lies here with grave unmarked since the absence of truth in evidence belies its owner's vault but that there may be traces found about his life as a spy, a brawler, a heretic, a magician, a homosexual, a duelist, a tobacco-user, a counterfeiter and my personal favorite – a rakehell – variously defined as a licentious or dissolute man of which I hold no doubt he was as some accounts reckon he was killed in a bawdy house, while others claim his death was punishment for heresy…but whatever the case, one must admit that death by being stabbed in the right eye is certainly pause for worship among the poets of greatness.

Where lie the frail remains of Emily Dickinson whose life was one very extended bout with seclusion and delusion, often having fantasies of an imaginary lover; but her true devotion was grounded in the vague search for meaning, though she knew little of that in anything spiritual or physical, of the divine providence of faith and whose language evolved into a meaningless banter of ecstasy and disappointment and the expected spiraling downward into an assured doubt and uncertainty eventually codified in her demise to a disease involving a slow and painful death by nephritis of the blood vessels, a swelling of the kidneys, and the end of days beginning only just to begin to understand the age old wisdom of mother telling us to go outside and play.

In a darkened corner obscured from the harsh light of reality, dank and morose, within this atmosphere the dim and shadowy figures hunched over as if pondering some ancient text, a recipe or protocol that will lead one to a different place of fantasy and glory – of unimagined visions and dreamlike states where one's consciousness drifts languidly in and out of a mystical void of reflection and surreality and where the mind is no longer fettered by the body, be free as it were to roam and explore and imagine all of the aspects that transcend the usual constraints of person and place and here and now sit these three huddled and wheezing in the clouds of joy and unrestrained of self ...Coleridge, Shelley, and Keats...great poets are thee.

To achieve greatness, I suppose I could marry then lose my wife and shortly thereafter witness the death of my four children, I could lapse into depression, and be viewed after my death as a misanthrope, anti-intellectual, a cruel, and angry man; I might, should I try to, fail miserably at school, at personal finances, and marry my thirteen year old cousin and upon her untimely death pursue several failed romances, drift into an unremitting siege of depression, and die of alcohol poisoning at the ripe old age of forty – enough to save me a place at the foot of great poets.

Now, this may not make sense but words cannot ever form complete and universal meaning and convey intent to all...so it would appear these lines I have written are the strange and perverted musings collected as if I had walked slowly down a corridor of an institution which for their own well-being houses those diagnosed with chronic depression whereupon is written the diagnostic narrative: *occupation*: poet; *relationships*: tenuous; *place in history*: unknown; and *prognosis*: doubtful – and regrettably what will be most likely, their final hurrah.

The truth is that I have reached a conundrum that by writing this...I acknowledge the inherent flaws...but by a creative and personal attempt to be a part of that strange admixture of personality and presentation, that I am now a part of that assorted and strange group who I have just examined...and here is the center of the issues...the real heart of the nature of art, what stands representational of what our civilizations gather up, save, and honor as anthems of religion, art, politics, culture...and ultimately our poetry.

In defense of art...by that I mean all art...there will always be issues of context, and reality, and those thorny problems which have to do with value as in good and bad, acceptable and outré, and that which ultimately outlives or survives the onslaught of emerging conditions of an ever evolving human environment capable of making many long held values obsolete or terribly simplistic which might have been the very impetus of da Vinci to note – *the poet ranks far below the painter in the representation of visible things* – so critical a comment as to make anyone – poet or artist cringe, become enuretic, to pound one's temples in disgust to think that membership at the altar of great poets could come at such a cost.

So it is that we might be slaves to our own delusions of insight, or perspective, of precious intellect and prowess...to which we owe the blind Milton some elevated and high flown respect wherein he writes in what may have been his own greatest creation, his last recollection and chronicled epiphany *Paradise Lost* now hardly read nor little understood by today's scholars who descry the lack of a video reproduction or wallpaper backdrop to accompany this work on the new anthology know as *YouTube*...and will never see nor hear those fiery words of remorse and failure echoed by Satan – *which way I fly is Hell, myself am Hell* – and that is the ultimate and sad demise of the form of art and of my dream to have a blessed and noble seat beside the great poets of the ages...but so it goes...*consummatum est*!

Solitude

Words are interesting in so many more ways, likely most people understand or ever will because they act upon our world, our ventures, and our lives in unusual and unexpected ways such that they are capable of being articulated in every manner from the literal to the extremely nuanced…and at that to such an incredible extent that they are very much like other relative human manifestations such as shadows, traits, accents, habits, capabilities, and all the sometimes wonderful and oftentimes insufferable ways of existence.

There are so many mysteries of life, of one's own life, of one's own destiny and direction – and this is to distinguish the point from commentary and exploratory exchange regarding life in general as in terms of biology or the cosmic consequences or any of an hundred or thousand or more venues of examining what appears to be and in fact is such a broad issue – so, to return to the original theme of life as defined more narrowly as that set of complex circumstances through which all of us travel at least to some degree or another, this is what happens.

One would think, as at least I have, that as time and age roll forward that each of us who is a genuine stakeholder in the realm of living and growing is reasonably happy, healthy, and prosperous; but put in the simplest of sentiments, life simply means an intimacy in all the pleasures and problems over a protracted period generally free for the most part of personal devastation, inexorable hardship, overwhelming disaster, abject poverty of spirit and mind, and the total destruction of any trace of hope, will find forgiveness, and redemption.

I have always tried as best I could to chart my course even from the earliest stumbling of education where for me in particular the childhood hardships included an inability to speak English clearly, to boast being raised in a prominent family of doctors, professors, bankers, or artists of renown, and an unmistakable yearning for assimilation along with what I had so often repeatedly heard both at home and elsewhere, the attainment of the "American Dream" which to my uniformed mind only meant the amassing of wealth and property.

If there were a keystone or foundational block or even an historical trace that might be a piece of the amalgam or an ancient cultural mix that colors me, marks me, and signifies me as to who or why I am or might be, the clues might lie in the twin forces of religion and extirpation – at it just might be that in that horrific period visited upon Armenians that something in nature or above saw fit to sow the seeds for my own life and as such justify the reason for my genesis should I dare to look upon myself and my path as favoring my soul over the material yet gaining both.

There are certain related maxims that owe their gravity to the stories inscribed in the *Old and New Testaments*; others, to the natural and nurturing lore of parents, the recombined efforts embedded with every cultural and societal moral fabric, and echoed in the other generalizations of maturing that occur say in education, in family, in all other relationships – interpersonal and otherwise – and reflected in our literature, art, music, and the primitive foot print that alleges we are human, civil, and charitable...and here is what puzzles most.

Yet, what is most distinct about this collection of words...yes, back to the original intrigue and conundrum of language...is that all of these aspects of our constructed, ordered, and codified human communication apparatus seem to carry the same flawed gene that is marked by how one might interpret meaning, intent, or implementation at any instance which is of course at the heart of this particular problem of confusion, of false starts, of promises failed, of hopes dashed, of emotions that rise and fall like the swells of the sea and matter little to anyone in the end.

Here is the core...that of the consequence which gnaws at me now and is manifested as a perversion of the noble abstraction of truth, and faith...which no longer can be trusted to be the marked representation of that by which the original intent...some true meaning or feeling that was once defined as love or certitude or caring...and from the earliest time had been created…if ever once was such the case…that we who call ourselves humanity might co-exist…but even that notion is dashed by the consistent failure of brotherhood and charity.

And again to the books, one only need examine the lives of Cain and Abel, of the wickedness of the sons of Judah, of the failure of trust and value of Jacob and Esau, of the discordant shame of power and lust that drove David against Uriah, and so…in the nature of the different choices I have made – and many of those not of my own creation – I have spent my life trying to set a course that would be, as much as possible, satisfactory and safe but that of course is little more that a wan hope given the disgusting habit of the intrusive nature of others.

But in age and wisdom I have learned that the most difficult ordeal one must face is patience, that out of patience will grow understanding, serenity, and resolution; that to struggle against a tide of characters who bring with them their own plagues and problems only to willingly make their strife contagious; to vaunt themselves or to find a perverse satisfaction by spreading their disease so that their own imminent demise is in some way shared and viewed as diminished; this echoes the wisdom of the ages, *thus it was early revealed to me to suffer fools gladly, seeing ye yourselves are wise.*

As for myself, I truly believe one element of life for me as measured in terms of true happiness is weighed not by the number of people one associates with, but the genuine quality and commitment of those associations; and here as with everything else in what we know of nature is that sometimes, our orbits must recognize that the possibility of colliding with those of others' can cause cataclysmic strife and change of polarity, path, and fortune…that all these can and do function strongly as to where our lives will go…and that for better or for worse.

Then, as I look back and muse over what has been an interesting history fraught with the nether regions of emotion and convergences of touching at times at the threshold of death, that now as I look forward eagerly, I realize that belief that *no man is an island unto itself* is only partially true; and, that I have more than done my best to share myself as *a part of the main* and perhaps effective in change within a world that is in chaos...so now, I dedicate myself, my time, my sense, and my art should any of these have any real viability...

And, therefore, I promise the remainder of my existence to my own private and self-satisfying days enjoying forever my metaphorical island of solitude and that in a permanent state of grace.

Thoughts on the Nature of Reading

A friend happened to ask the other day what I have been reading...?
I thought to myself, *"The Journal of the Tour to the Hebrides* by Johnson and Boswell
Which I found extremely entertaining...a joy to read" I believe I replied.

"And what are you reading now...if anything at all?" my friend continued.
"The Selected Letters of D. H. Lawrence consisting of three hundred missives
Which makes one wonder just how many there were...and what of those left out?"

And it is this that got me to thinking curiously about the nature of reading;
Why do many people no longer bother to read...at least anything serious...
And why, instead, do those many people gravitate towards visual delights?

Might it be the case that "reading" requires a necessary expenditure of imagination,
Or that "reading" involves an exercise wholly connected to and engaged with words;
And that "reading" consists of an active and conscious intellectual curiosity?

What puzzles most is that no amount of scientific research will be able to fathom
Why reading has become out of the main, an adventure lost on modern society,
A once-treasured activity now seemingly tossed aside like an old childhood toy.

Where once those youthful dreams saw fulfillment in the imaginings of stories,
In times when children's fantasies ran freely as on hills and valleys and visions
Painted in words of poets and authors and musicians whose lyric form was my world.

To walk in a dream state the western dales and shores, the inland valleys, and barren 'scape
As that drawn about the Hebrides – the bitter cold, the primitive hut, the remains of the past;
To marvel at the rugged coastline, its blustery winds, its roiling sea, its unforgiving nature.

And read as if in some voyeuristic way a person's letters…so full of life and frustration,
Fusing at once the poverty of the soul, the aching desire for love, the desperate hope for life;
Yet, always the nagging insistence of failure and obsession over loss and inevitability.

Thus, it might be that the nature of reading has become difficult for modern society,
Whose inhabitants now face other realities, other hardships, other uncertainties in life;
Too much is it to task that imagination to squander on vicarious activities of the lives of others.

Better to let pictures be made for digestion like formula, recombined visions of vitality
Where imagination boundless as it may be is held in check to stay the hopes of what may be;
That primitive, articulate, hungry, vengeful, desire, child of responsibility may not appear.

The nature of reading is then relegated to those few who dare to venture into their own creation,

An imagined voyage along open seas, vast lands of eternity, all fraught with danger and illusion;

Yet, a delight at every turn for the sojourner who views every piece of literature as a fine frigate.

Tramp Stamp

As I recollect, the first time I noticed this particularly curious tattoo
was early morning
While browsing the array of vegetables so pristinely laid out at
Safeway each dewy fresh,
Like the tart and ripe youthfulness who stood before me a thong
pulled high above her hips
As if to notify one and all who near and far might take heed of her
personal brand of self.

It was here, roaming idly among the tomatoes, artichokes, cucumbers,
and the rest that
I first thought about my friend Allen Ginsberg's musings about
homoeroticism among the fruit,
In San Francisco mulling over the herbal selection and connecting
this to some arcane search for
The soul of Walt Whitman into the "neon fruit supermarket dreaming
of your enumerations."

It was Mayfair Market at San Jose and Ocean long since re-christened
now a community church.
Once, open twenty-four hours it nurtured the tormented spirits as the
customers came in shifts;
Where two to four were the hungry dopers, four to five the grim
castoffs suffering for sustenance
Roaming in shaggy solitude for anything that might stave off death
for a moment at fifteen cents.

It was when gaudiness and perversion were closeted and the denizens
flitted in their own light;
Yet, now so changed where every label owns a cachet; and it could
be anything from a birthright
Sold for nothing to body art that displays affiliation or self or a decree
or other such vestige that
Social insects do seek today perhaps to be counted or stand above or
find their nature's lure.

Most American cities have a Chinatown which is usually an eerie admixture of historical reality;
The signs and signals of disenfranchisement meant to disguise the shame of cultural abdication.
One may visit here and there to discover long forgotten relics buried by years of subjugation,
Transplantation, hegemony, colonialism, forced ghettoization, adumbration, and marginalization.

All the artifacts which declare *Made in Japan*, *Fabrique en Chine*, *Hecho en Mexico* and so on,
Stir in me, at least, odious pronouncements of the kinds of artificiality that serve as engines of
Long suffering economies, values really, that have died and faded from memory no longer real;
That they must carry their own advertisements, their statements of who and what and wherefore.

In this view, these tin, ceramic, fake leather, faux fur and slipshod children of third world models
Are the new orphans soon to become whores as they adjust and find their own special niche in
Modernity…a time and place which has left them behind, just ignorant and bereft enough;
Where their identity is shaped by bewildering assortments of garish clothing and body markings.

So it is I see these newly minted tramp stamps ornate as a cathedral window and as commodious,
As symmetrical as an engineered interstate freeway, as perfectly coded as any high tech runway;
Could, if it should find the need or if it please, guide a Zeppelin delicately into its hangar and yes
That is what compels one to query what purpose does this blueprint serve than as a tramp ramp?

Where beg indulgences from the phalanx of nuns and priests and the echoing admonition and
Emerging from the confessional impure thoughts these declarations on the backsides do conjure,
Of the young girls, and all the rest of the seeming desperate legion of wanton women ignorant
Not seeing their purchase of self-promotion in a mocking feminism of the twenty-first century?

Seemingly despite time and experience and even the winds of change, women remain as weary
And as enigmatic as the ancient ring of Gyges...in this new resurrection of fad or fashion;
Are they actually announcing, would they have any need to, that they are the repository of life,
As modern technology has so disrupted natural behavior that they must show us where to enter?

Ultimately and what I find most intriguing is that I might live long enough to see a time when,
If such a thing were possible, the end of procreation would be at hand no more left to the messy
Slogging about of courtship, with its ancient dances and feints, its false hopes or dead-end paths
All relegated to the scientific pragmatism where the ramp guides tubes, dishes, and humanity.

Uncle Arthur at Lavabo

Who can ever fathom why some memories seem to be burned into
one's personal history
Or as important become a solid shape of a remembrance that is set
upon a shelf of the mind
A part one might simply regard a beloved family member at a random
gathering of moment
That for this own special reason gather themselves into this unique
recollection?

Uncle Arthur was married for life to *Bazmen*, my aunt where they
lived in a glorious simplicity
On North Maple near the college, immaculate and wide and lined
neatly with Sycamore trees!
Why was it called Maple? It was one of those houses that has a broad
porch and sloping roof
With obligatory dormers, a driveway of thin cement strips and evenly
neat lawn between them.

But here is the part that may seem most interesting at least to me and
if truth be told and written
As it occurred and related to any psychoanalyst, psychologist, or
other so-called student of those
Allied sciences that would hope to probe, map and make sense of this
very remembrance and if,
They could provide an answer or a reason or at minimum a purpose
to this germ of a thought.

So this is the image; at around four in the afternoon, every day, Uncle
Arthur positioned himself
As carefully as the captain of a ship in front of the small mirror of a
door to the medicine cabinet
In a bathroom the size of a jail cell and cluttered with hampers, tub,
toilette, and racks of towels.
Razor in hand, skin taut, chin outstretched, scanning the landscape
of the face as a blank canvas.

Uncle Arthur has completed a very close shave etching artfully his own Charley Chan moustache
At most two inches wide a third of an inch thick and here he takes the greatest pride and time or
Exercise in primping this area…it is then he applies the light and airy handfuls of *Aqua Velva*
To those cheeks and intones deeply…aaaaah…as if in ritual and necessary custom of response.

Uncle Arthur was a rare individual who at age fifty was as handsome as say William Powell…
Or perhaps Basil Rathbone but I was a child of five or six and my references are murky at best
As I align reality in this musing would state he had about ten, maybe twelve, or… perhaps fifteen
Strands of slick black hair as straight as the commandments and as obedient as the lambs of God.

It was here he would commit to his own baptism anointing his head with the unction of *Vitalis,*
Scenting the confined shrine of ablution with an aroma of perfume and masculine alcohol like a
Medieval chemist or conjuror might produce the aura of mystery and precisely for me at age five
Exists as a significant episode in my own life and connects this memory as a notion of love.

Lingering ideas and thoughts of both time and place are as important in the assay of who we are
Or who we might be in those we cannot clearly define a place and significance in our own lives;
But that is simply, and at this time and place, not as important in knowing for certain and why…
It is simply better to think on those memories as children of the mind and the vestiges of respect.

189

Yellow Fever

I was about eight or nine when I first recollect I even saw or felt yellow fever although of course it was not identified by that in terms of forensic or pathogenic ways since to me the abstract "fever" illness was not yet known nor plainly understood.

Ranches and fields of crops are often set apart by what are called windbreakers, a row of Eucalyptus trees or a thick gorse of hedge that protect the tender crops from fierce weather and other stray and alien elements.

Let us here get some facts out front and these are that as the only male born to the family and the last at that, one commandment was the declaration that I would unequivocally marry an Armenian girl if such a soul actually were in existence.

If…and that is a vastly huge supposition…such an one of a creature be discovered, her distinct rarity of an occasion would be tantamount to say the finding of the Ark of the Covenant or some other such relic of high distinction and relative holiness.

And let this be understood that were such a creature found among the layered issues of history, the bands of epochs, and the striation of sheer time, that such a person would be considered as rare a find as the crown of thorns and most likely just as painful.

Elevated in speech as this might seem, there exists no hyperbole nor exaggeration for those children of God cradled in the Caucasus and born of the first Christian realm who were indeed as elusive as a woman's desire and as mysterious as the Dead Sea Scrolls.

To be sure, these unusual and nubile creatures were in every sense possessed of a dual aspect of nature…one, their numbers were infinitesimally small and two, their futures surely lay in antipodal realms away from Armenian boys…and I was one.

Thus, to the point that for me, at any rate, my life was charted quite early as choices in the potential pool of female candidates had thinned itself out much the way nature culls its fringe element players and runts of the litters.

For me, however, the "fever" began vicariously in the vague and mist-filled novels of Conrad who hovered precariously far up into the waterways of Malaya, deep into his heart of darkness along the jagged and timeless coastlines of the China Sea.

Swept off at youth, innocence, and an unindulged fervor of youthful heat and wanton lust, I was taken to islands in unknown archipelagoes, on strands of shores where small breasted brown skinned women gathered water or washed their clothes on rocks.

Days and weeks were filled with narratives so dramatically painted in thick and textured description so compelling that young men with otherwise assured futures abandoned reality and took up the siren call of the sea.

Heaven bless the ancient lore of stories of voyages of the great Ulysses and Jason and the scores of others who plied their life and married fortunes in such adventures to foreign lands and mystical climes.

It is not a great leap of either faith or imagination to wistfully dream as does youth or act as does the man to seek out such exotic environments that are the lairs where dwells the contagion of "yellow fever" so favored in ballad and in recollection.

The "fever" seems, if one is to follow historical documentaries, pandemic...yet, while no one died, many were sickened in heart by the stings and darts and the deeply felt pains and pangs of remembrances of love's lost effort drying up on a faraway shore.

There are unfortunately many painful chapters or interruptions that are a necessary part of the complicated weaving of such a seemingly whimsical tale of love and the oddly bizarre struggle between reality and hope which never seem to find resolution.

My very first encounter was, I believe, at an early and most innocent time in my life when I was about six or seven still learning English under the tyranny of a chorus of guttural utterances of those around me who spoke Armenian and some in the family considered the language of Jesus!

I remember it all vividly as I lay sprawled out on the carpet with the Sunday paper before me, the funny pages as we knew them, with their colorful panels arrayed neatly as if life's episodes were ever really like that.

I often took refuge in front of what seemed to me at that time an enormous Zenith radio as tall as my sister and as broad as Aunty Aghavni, admired by all for her ample hips and her ability to produce children as easily as Ford produced cars...but I digress.

The earliest onset of "yellow fever" owed its genesis to a character who was so beautiful and mysterious that I was unable to discern the inherent evil that lay beneath her surface even though I could read and make sense of the nature of her portrayal.

She was evil...part witch, part siren, part seductress...her eyes sparkling through half closed lids, beautifully arched brows owing their architectural curve to God alone, and above, a curtain of shiny black hair as straight and even as church pews.

My mind fixated on that face which revealed nothing; and when if by great fortune her entire self might be seen, her body wrapped in silk from chin to toe top, a choking mandarin collar and a seamless package of the finest cloth sheer and as tight as sausage casing.

She carried herself like a goddess, she was as erect as the columns of ancient Greece, she had a bearing that insisted itself upon and above all else, and her perfectly shaped breasts forced themselves as sculpted buttresses meant as much for protection as allure.

Her name or more accurately her title, since as I recall she never was addressed by any other, was "Dragon Lady"...which I believed to be

192

a perfectly appropriate declaration since anything less would have been too common and thus beneath her station.

That bout of "fever" stayed with me over a period of time since none I encountered could come close to the elusive beauty she carried about her; there were many young girls; yet, they never quite held up to my iconic villainess of *Terry and the Pirates*.

There was Marian Koyano whose face was all the beauty and grace as reflected in Kenko's poetry, the antiquity of the *Heian Period*, her simple smile all down cast eyes owing much to the probable sweetness of her young heart.

But her figure was all one in shape, graceless, formless, indistinct and most likely good for labor or for the unending constancy of bearing children, bent over, performing with regularity the rituals of motherhood and growing old like a persimmon tree.

There was by stark contrast Leslie Nosé, daughter of a man who had lost everything only to emerge in a new and more prosperous venue as first a lowly gardener and then a fine and accomplished landscape designer as he was described by his number one daughter.

She represented herself more like a starlet, her hair short like Sophia Loren, her lithe body thin as a chow mein noodle, never a smile on equally thin lips which if ever parted would reveal teeth the color of a morning fog.

Lastly, there was among this parade another who might rise some day and perhaps with more subtlety of breeding and self-awareness and could be comparable in beauty as those possessed by my "Dragon Lady".

Her name was Ruby Nakasone and it suited her well; she reminded me of a slick Japanese dive bomber, with a gleaming fuselage, and nearly flawless symmetry, a geometry of purpose, and a mouth painted so red it could strike terror in the soul of man.

My times with "yellow fever" would come and go as regularly as the ebb and flow of the Pacific or as beautifully violent as rogue waves in the Sea of Japan, each encounter an examination of the physical and cultural artifacts that were an essential part of each candidate.

Perhaps the worst case of the "fever" struck me during a most vulnerable and volatile time in my life when I served a tour of duty in the "Pearl of the Orient" – a surreal place of endless rice paddies, thick and verdant jungles, and villages as ancient as time itself.

It was mercifully inhabited by a profuse and profound garden of almond-eyed beauties who perpetually dressed night or day, at work or at leisure in black silk pajamas which hung casually and carelessly about their bodies and without pretense.

The cloth seemed to be a part of them as if from birth like some soft smooth chrysalis which flowed refulgently in the breeze and clung to their bodies as naturally as babies to mothers evoking wonder and a nascent mystery which lay just beneath the surface of the character.

Everything about them spoke economy, not of expense but of a much higher state as inartistic representation…nothing overdone, every detail fragrant as if some artisan who owes a loyalty and obligation to exact from that unsculpted rock an end goal of great beauty.

I have reflected upon the divides that seem to evidence the differences between East and West; the representing of women as ample breasted, callipygian, eyes wide and glaring, wearing expressions that hide their secret contempt for men and perhaps themselves.

But those of whom I speak whose pandemic "fever" I have known and suffered are manifestly separate, their lovely eyes turned aside, their hair arranged as clearly as a flower garden, their breasts unseen beckoning because they are not seen, their hue as that of rarest orchids.

The notion of "yellow fever" fascinates because like issues which confront men, whether intentional or not, no matter what we might believe we know and understand, we are forever and inevitably children guided by imagination on the path in search of our "Dragon Lady".